Telephone

The 7 Keys of
Charisma

For my Mother
who knows a great deal about charismatics
With Love

The 7 Keys of
Charisma

Joanna Kozubska

YOURS TO HAVE AND TO HOLD
BUT NOT TO COPY

First published in 1997

Kogan Page Limited
120 Pentonville Road
London N1 9JN

British Library Cataloguing in Publication Data
A CIP record for this book is available from the British Library.
ISBN 0 7494 2116 9

Typeset by Northern Phototypesetting Co. Ltd., Bolton
Printed in England by Clays Ltd, St Ives plc

CONTENTS

ACKNOWLEDGEMENTS

This book is a team effort.

Dr Aubrey Wilson first suggested I should write a book. Karen Jackson gave me the first title, 'How to be sh... hot and charismatic' (which we all decided we couldn't use for obvious reasons). Jo Denby came up with a new title, 'The Keys of Charisma.' My agent Mandy Little encouraged me to write it, found Kogan Page for me and, when I was feeling very low, helped me to continue. Karen Hargreaves sent out and collated the questionnaires and responses, and organised and transcribed most of the interviews for me. Mary Brown and Kay Bradley helped with the latter. My friends, clients, and several hundred other people, who sadly must remain nameless, filled in the questionnaires and sent them back to me. Many friends lent me books and collected relevant cuttings for me. Dr Sian Baverstock started my research by giving me all her material on leadership to read. Dr Gill Hanscombe and Dr Suniti Namjoshi taught me so much about writing, through their own work, through discussion and through answers to my specific questions. Jeremy Draper put up with my technical incompetence and answered my cries for help at all times of the day and night. Sue Draper found information for me, retrieved chapters I'd inadvertently erased and worked with me all the way with great good humour and at times often inconvenient to herself. My friends at the Buckingham Book Shop met all my requests for books with interest and kindness. The London Library produced the obscure for me. Kim Hodge corrected my French, and with her friends chased quotations for me. Jenny Quantrell introduced me to her learning set, and together with Karen Jackson, Clare Denby, Chris Hoardley and my sister Danuta, read chapters and said just the right things. Sue De Verteuil focused my mind by cutting through the fog to help me when I had to cut the manuscript by a third. Liana Guy listened and listened and listened to all my doubts about the book for 18 months. My editor, Susan Pollock, and her colleagues at Kogan Page gave me the professional help I needed to complete the task.

My most grateful thanks must go to Jo Denby. I could not have written the book without all her help and support. She has lived every page with me!

DRAMATIS PERSONAE

Sir Antony Acland GCMG	Provost of Eton
Major General Sir John Acland KCB CBE DL	Farmer
Maureen Acland OBE	Chairman, Council of the Queen's Nursing Institute
Benedict Allen	Explorer
Tony Buzan	Author of 44 books, Inventor of Mind Maps, Co-founder of the Mind Sports Olympiad
Edwina Currie MP	Politician and Author
Jean-Marie Descarpentries	Chairman and CEO, Groupe Bull, Paris
Fred Dibnah	Steeplejack
Christine Dipple	Headmistress, Talbot Heath School
Dame Rennie Fritchie DBE	Hon Visiting Professor, York University, Chair in Creative Leadership
Evelyn Glennie OBE	Solo and Percussionist
Pia Helena Ormerod	Director, Swedish Chamber of Commerce for the United Kingdom
Sir John Harvey Jones	Author, Consultant and Industrialist
Robert Heller	Author, Consultant and Management Guru
Cynthia Homer	Retired Teacher, Cheltenham Ladies' College
Grethe Hooper Hanson	Director, SEAL
Lieutenant General Mike Jackson CBE MBE	Commander, Allied Command Europe, Rapid Reaction Corps
Barry John	Sportsman and Rugby Player
Stephen Johnson	Group Chairman, Coutts Consulting Group Plc
Paul Lever	Chairman, Ashworth Hospital Authority, Chairman, BSM Group Plc
Baroness Jill Pitkeathley OBE	Chief Executive, Carers National Association

Heather Rabbatts	CEO, Lambeth Borough Council
Peter Sharpe QPM	Chief Constable, Hertfordshire
Rev Peter Timms OBE	Director, TIME ...
Les Williams	Consultant
Dr Gordon Wills	Principal, International Management Centres
Dr Aubrey Wilson	Consultant and Marketing Guru
Nancy Wise	Broadcaster, Communications Consultant

INTRODUCTION

On his first visit to my school in the four years I had been there, my father kissed the hand of my rather formidable headmistress in full view of my friends and their families. A rather gauche teenager, I nearly died with embarrassment. No one else's father behaved like this. What really startled me was that she didn't appear to mind at all – far from it!

As a small child I thought that my father was wonderful. People told me that he was a war hero, which of course made him even more special. He was good-looking, bearded and spoke with a very heavy Polish accent which enthralled many. Following a career in the Polish cavalry, the French resistance and then the Polish squadron of RAF Bomber Command, with a Polish VC, a Croix De Guerre and a DFC, he 'swashbuckled' his way through life talking the hind legs off several herds of donkeys and putting grandiose ideas into action. Some ideas were successful. Some were disastrous. People either hated or loved him. Few saw him objectively. For many, he made their dreams come alive. For others, he brought a touch of romance to their lives. And others he damaged, often irreparably.

He was the first truly charismatic person I met.

Laying some of the ghosts to rest and coming to terms with a larger-than-life parent has taken a long time, and writing this book is part of the process. I have inherited some of his characteristics, as have my sisters. All of us have been called charismatic, but we do not have the same level of charisma as him. I wanted a much greater understanding of a charismatic personality and I wanted to understand what made him tick – what we had inherited.

I have been attracted by charismatic personalities throughout my career, and I am still intensely motivated by charismatic people. In writing this book I set out to understand the phenomenon in greater depth and to understand it against the background of my own world, the world of management development. I set out feeling that many of the things that charismatics did – how they behaved, how they dealt with situations – were very effective, and I wanted to know if this effect could be replicated. What were their strengths and what were their weaknesses? Could this incredible gift that some people are given be learned? If we did not have it, could we develop it? What were the pitfalls and dangers?

I wanted to know what other people thought about charisma. What did people understand by the term? Do we all think the same? Who are the great charismatics of the past and of the present? I sent out a questionnaire to 700 people and received a superb response. I selected the recipients at random in a number of areas: the military, the church, politicians, journalists and media folk, management consultants, health service professionals, educationalists, school children, MBA students and … my Christmas card list! True, there were lots of gaps. I did not set out to do a rigorous, scientifically based statistical study and indeed, have not done so. I am more interested in the qualitative information than anything else.

I asked people a number of questions:

- What does the word 'charismatic' mean to you?
- Who would you describe as charismatic (alive or dead)?
- Who would you describe as a charismatic leader?
- Who would you describe as charismatic (but not as a leader)?

I also asked them to describe themselves using a tick list. I wanted to get some impression of the kind of people who identified charismatic people. Did they appear to be a particular personality type?

I had an amazing 35 per cent response rate to my questionnaire and suspect that I have been provided with unique feedback on the popular view of what constitutes charisma. I have included a representative selection of statements describing charisma at the end of the book. It is interesting to note that by far the majority of respondents saw charisma as a positive quality. The words most frequently used to describe charismatic individuals included 'inspiring, energy, vision, follow, leadership, charm, passion, communication, direction and confidence'.

Many people said that they found the concept fascinating, describing some of the discussions they had had as interesting, stimulating and even confrontational! As a result of the information received I wrote to a number of those identified as charismatic and asked if I could come and interview them. Naturally many felt unable to help me, which is perfectly understandable. A number sent me very kind words. Those featured in the book gave me their time and their confidence for which I am so very grateful. The experience of meeting such a wide range of remarkable people has been a privilege and one for which I shall always be thankful. Without them I could not have contemplated writing this book. Charisma does lie 'in the eye of the beholder' and, as we shall see, not all of the people I met were charismatic according to my own definition. But I did find almost all of them all to be remarkable people. Most gave me much more than the time I asked for and I was entertained royally on a number of occasions. I am indebted to them all. I am particularly grateful to Tony Buzan who gave me a great deal of encouragement and invited me to his Mind Sports Olympiad in August this year. I have used extracts from the interviews to illustrate my views and those of the people I interviewed throughout the book, in what I hope are appropriate places.

My next task was to write the book. By nature I am very 'right-brained'. Although I have acquired some discipline in my thinking and am reasonably analytical when I need to be, left to my own devices my thought patterns tend to be unstructured and rather serendipitous. I have followed my instincts and, to a large extent, my book reflects unexpected and happy accidents of discovery and things remembered. This will be very irritating for some of my readers but I hope that I have traced some lines of enquiry in a more structured and detailed way to enable them to stay with me. It is highly likely that I have missed things which seem obvious and that my research is incomplete. However, I feel that the topic is never-ending in its fascination, and I had to stop somewhere!

Although I researched charisma extensively I have not included an in-depth study of the concept in this book, preferring to reflect what I personally found out about the quality from both my own experience and that of my interviewees. When planning this book, I had hoped to include chapters based on interviews with the three individuals who received the most 'charismatic' nominations – Lady Thatcher, Nelson Mandela and Richard Branson. Unfortunately I was not able to meet them.

Despite the horrors which have been perpetrated by one or two notable charismatics, Adolf Hitler, for example, I find myself convinced that charisma is something very special. Those who have good measure of this magic dust, this gift, have so much to offer and we would all be the poorer without them. But charisma is not a gift for the few. We all have it and, if we are not afraid of it, we can develop and use it for the benefit of others and ourselves.

And what of my father now? I understand him a little better. I also have a much greater understanding of the reasons for my own fascination with charismatics.

Joanna Kozubska
Buckingham

BEFORE YOU READ ON...

I wrote this book hoping that, at the very least, it will give you some new ideas on how you might increase your managerial and leadership effectiveness. At best, it will provide you with a structure for a personal development plan.

At the front of each of the seven 'Keys of Charisma' chapters you will find a questionnaire designed to start you thinking about the Key concerned. You will find the scoring system at the end of each questionnaire.

Chapter 5 explores how you might draw up a personal development plan. You are asked to plot your questionnaire scores on the Charismatic Start chart you will find within this chapter. If you choose to plot the scores you might give a particular role model for the same Key on the Star as well, then you will have a target to aim for in each Key area.

If you do nothing else, have fun completing the questionnaires!

PART 1

CHARISMA IN CONTEXT

WHO WANTS TO BE CHARISMATIC AND MEMORABLE ANYWAY?

1

'Would you like to be a manager like me, helping to run a big factory? Or work in an office managing people's money like Mummy?'

'Oh no. That's borrrring!'

A recent survey among school children asked them what careers they would choose if all were open to them. Their responses included pop star, doctor, lawyer, astronaut, the military, the fire service, footballer and actor. When asked why none of them had selected industry or commerce, the response came back – 'That's borrrrrrring!'

In the survey I conducted internationally for the purposes of this book, I asked individuals from a wide range of occupations who they considered to be charismatic. With one or two notable exceptions the vast majority of responses identified politicians, actors, writers, religious leaders, cult figures, sports personalities, journalists and royalty. Why so few industrialists? Why so few managers? Why have managers and industrialists apparently failed to make much impact on us? Do we, like the children, feel that these occupations are boring and, by implication, that the people associated with them are boring too? The notable exceptions were Sir John Harvey Jones and Richard Branson of the Virgin Group. What have they got that the others do not have? According to the survey – charisma. For many they are inspiring, successful and refreshing. They break the mould.

Charismatic people are successful and memorable. No bad thing if you are in a management role of any kind. The ability to make a positive impact if you are going for an interview for a new job or promotion, if you are in sales or business development, or if you have to make presentations, will go a long way to achieving your objectives. Charisma is a very useful attribute if you want to make an impact.

Two recent studies, one from America and one from the UK, suggest that the most successful CEOs attribute much of their success to their ability to use attributes associated with the right side of their brain rather than their left. This includes their ability to juggle several balls in the air at once (most women do this very well!) and to synthesise rather than analyse, their communication skills, their intuition, visioning, empathy and sensitivity. The majority of charismatic individuals have all these attributes.

As managers and CEOs, how good are we at identifying charismatic people within our organisations, nurturing them – and keeping them within the system? There is plenty of evidence to suggest that we get rid of visionaries and 'movers and shakers' who do not always conform to our way of thinking. Michael Kami, an American management guru, describes these people as guerrillas. Unfortunately, organisations also tend to see them as gorillas! And so out they go. Charismatic people have different thoughts and ideas. Ideas that are the stuff of tomorrow. We push them out – and they set up in competition!

Many of today's most successful sales people are intensely charismatic. They achieve dramatic results and their secrets must surely be worth learning. As sales folk or managers ourselves responsible for business results, we must surely be interested in the part charisma plays in successful selling. The amazing success of the multilevel marketing organisations such as Amway and Mary Kay rest on the charisma of their founders and on their ability to institutionalise their approach and attract other charismatic individuals to join them. There has to be much for us to learn and use in our own organisations.

In their book *Managing Without Management*, Richard Koch and Ian Godden suggest that large organisations have become far too complicated. They are being strangled by their own management processes. They suggest that six ever more powerful forces will dispense with management as we know it today – power from customers, information, investors, global markets, simplicity and leadership. These six forces are unstoppable. They see the emergence of a new breed of superleaders, not managers, to deal with this very different world. These superleaders do not use the management hierarchy to impose their will. They use five other techniques: charisma and force of personality; value-based culture and propaganda; industry knowledge and insight; computer-based control; and unpredictability or continuous revolution. For Koch and Godden, Richard Branson of Virgin, Bill Gates of Microsoft and Jack Welsh of GE epitomise the kind of superleaders we need. All three of these were identified as charismatic in my survey.

What is charisma? It is a gift, an energy, an ability to inspire others with vision and make things happen. It can be a positive gift, or it can be very dangerous and destructive to others. Can it be learned? We may not be able to learn to be charismatic *per se*, but we can identify particular behaviours that appear to achieve the results we desire. For example, how can we become a very successful leader and manager rather than just a leader and manager? How can we make sure that our achievements and contributions live on after we have gone? How can we leave a memorable impression behind us when we are interviewed for a new job or promotion? How can we ensure that our sales calls are really effective and that our clients or customers look forward to seeing us again? How can we ensure that we make memorable and effective presentations?

Can we increase our own effectiveness? One way is to look at the role models and examples all around us. Many of the most successful people today *are* charismatic, and it is their charisma that makes them stand out above others in their field. Their charisma attracts people to them so that they do indeed achieve their goals.

What can we learn from charismatic individuals? How can an understanding of their charisma and its effect upon others help each one of us? Chapter 2 explores the nature of charisma. Each one of us has both the potential and the opportunity to develop charismatic behaviours if we think that these would be beneficial. We all have the choice and I make the assumption that few people would actively choose to be forgotten. Charisma is one way to be remembered!

WHAT IS CHARISMA?

2

WHERE DID THE CONCEPT ORIGINATE?

No prizes for knowing that the word 'charisma' comes from the Greek.

The Greeks believed that charisma was an extraordinary gift of the gods, a favour, a talent, a divinely conferred power which gave recipients the capacity to inspire their followers with devotion and enthusiasm. The word charisma itself comes from the Greek word 'kharis' meaning favour, grace. The early Christian called individuals who claimed this divine inspiration 'charismatic', and these people tended to be the most important in the church. Charisma was still seen as a gift from a divine being, but in this case God himself rather than the many pagan gods. This understanding of 'charisma' and 'charismatic' is still alive and well today in the Christian church.

Bob Geldof – gift from God?

Mo Acland explored the idea of a gift from God in a modern setting.

> 'I was interested in the definition, "being God-given", something that is placed upon you or given to you in some way, not necessarily acquired. Can it be developed by virtue of having a platform? Sometimes this happens to people who you normally wouldn't think twice about. They achieve a position and a platform which gives them a certain innate confidence and something to say. It gives them a position in other people's view which creates this illusion of charisma.

> I am thinking, for instance, of Bob Geldof. If I met him in the street I wouldn't think he was charismatic, in fact I'd probably think, go home and brush your hair! And yet look what he achieved with Band Aid.'

Not all my interviewees were happy with the idea that charisma is God-given.

> 'It does not come from God. A lot of charisma means a lot of work, it's not a gift, you have to learn it.'
>
> *Jean-Marie Descarpentries*

There is little evidence of any major debate on the word charisma until the early twentieth century when Max Weber, a German, who was both a professor of law and a social scientist, examined the concept in some detail.

Charisma makes a unique and magical impact on others

For Max Weber, charisma was about extraordinariness and outstanding leadership. This element of extraordinariness led him to believe that charisma was applicable to gurus and world leaders rather than more ordinary folk. But, interestingly enough, he saw charisma as a force which would wane with the progress of the modern world, although there would always be times of distress when charismatic individuals would emerge.

Since Max Weber academics in Europe and the US have studied the concept in depth. It has become synonymous with leadership and it is in this context that most of the research and observation has been done, and I will touch on this in Chapter 3.

IN THE EYE OF THE BEHOLDER

It takes at least two people for one to be charismatic! Robinson Crusoe did not have a chance of being charismatic until Man Friday appeared. No one can be charismatic on their own. Charisma implies the existence of followers and is rather like beauty in that it lies 'in the eye of the beholder'. It goes without saying that an individual perceived as charismatic by one person may not be perceived as so by another, particularly when the perceivers, or audience, are very different in nature, with different ideas of 'beauty' or charisma. One has only to look at the list of people identified in the survey as charismatic to observe the truth of this! Many of the respondents reported enjoying much debate and discussion when completing their questionnaires. A real charismatic for one person was frequently identified as a 'total turn off' for others.

Lieutenant General Mike Jackson described charisma like this:

'I suppose if charisma means anything it means colour. It's pretty subjective; presumably it's in the eyes of the beholder. It's descriptive of somebody to whom others relate easily. It is an ability to carry people with you and to make it a fairly enjoyable experience for them and not a miserable one. It certainly isn't being dull or boring. People enjoy your company. You make life fun, you crack a joke, it's what you do with them and for them.'

Charisma is a word used to describe the qualities, behaviour and attitudes of someone else; it is not a description that we normally apply to ourselves, although we might agree that we have some of the characteristics implied by the word. Our reticence might, however, indicate a cultural bias. In my interviews with a wide range of European individuals identified as charismatic in the survey, most of them found it difficult to accept that they were seen by some as charismatic. However, they were prepared to agree that they had many charismatic behaviours. In contrast, much of the American literature would suggest that Americans find it easier to see themselves as charismatic.

'I don't think anyone can be charismatic in a vacuum. It has to be about the effect you have on other people and how people react to you. I think it has something to do with passion because I'm sure the only way I'm seen as charismatic is through the work that I do. I don't know that I'm seen as particularly charismatic in my personal life'.

Baroness Pitkeathley

Charisma is about magic and emotion. It is about the warm glow that we get from listening to truly charismatic individuals. It is about excitement, wonder and belief. We are *personally involved* when we identify anyone as charismatic. Benedict Allen, the explorer, agreed with this description.

'I think it's a sort of magic – a sort of invisible something or other. It's a power that someone has to draw others to them. For me, I think of magic whenever I think of charisma. I think of a sort of invisible bond somehow that this person is able to establish with another person.'

In addition to particular behaviours, charisma describes a social relationship in which followers give their loyalty and 'followership' in exchange for the benefits they want. The benefits they may be looking for might include a vision, a cause, deliverance, clear leadership, excitement or inspiration.

OK – let's talk about Hitler

It is difficult to have any discussion about charisma without Adolf Hitler's name being mentioned. He is always given as the reason why charisma is an undesirable quality to be avoided at all costs! I want to put Hitler into context and show that he is an example of one particular type of charismatic only. So where did he come from?

In a crisis people look for someone to rescue them, and the crisis itself prompts people to offer themselves as rescuer. The economic crises and social disorganisation in Germany in the 1930s certainly facilitated the appearance of Hitler. The majority of Germans saw him as someone able to deliver them from the economic and psychological distress prevailing in Germany after the First World War. Hitler's 'gift' of charisma was directly related to the crisis of the moment. The Germans wanted someone to deliver them from a situation which they felt was untenable. They wanted their self-respect back. Winston Churchill, who was often very unpopular both before and after the Second World War, fulfilled the same role in Britain. He too gave people what they wanted – strong leadership and the promise of deliverance from an evil enemy. The majority of the British people believed that he would lead Britain to victory and they were prepared to put their trust in him and, indeed, their lives in his hands.

Both Hitler and Churchill were men of the moment – a product of their times. They emerged as a result of the crises in Europe.

RETURN OF THE PRIMAL FATHER

It is difficult to understand how charismatic leaders such as Hitler and Jim Jones of the People's Temple Sect in Guyana were able to induce people to behave in ways which appear quite inexplicable. The mass extermination of millions and the induced mass suicide of 914 people is not to be contemplated by a civilised society. And yet it undoubtedly happened. It wasn't Hitler himself who closed the doors on the gas chambers. His followers, ordinary human beings, did that. What went wrong? Why did ordinary people suspend their own judgement and behave in ways which flew in the face of a civilised society? Freud (wouldn't you know it!) may have some of the answers. He suggests that one of the most appealing aspects of a strong leader is that 'They represent at an unconscious level the return of the primal father.' The theory goes on to suggest that followers replace conscious thinking with an unconscious version of the leader's thinking; this removes any conflict that they might have felt between the two. And so life becomes much easier and more comfortable. At the same time the followers project their wishes on to the leader in a very exaggerated way. They pass responsibility to the leader and the leader becomes their conscience. For example, at the Nuremberg Trials Goering claimed that Hitler had become his conscience.

Hitler and Jim Jones exemplify charismatic individuals at their very worst.

The attraction of cults

Religious cults normally have charismatic leaders who are seen as being able to meet their followers' psychological needs. The Reverend Sun Myung Moon of 'Moonies' fame is well known for the influence he exerts over his followers. Followers often come from unstable and troubled family backgrounds and, as a result, may be social misfits with a poor sense of personal identity. Their unhappiness and discomfort may indicate a deep sense of worthlessness, which prompts them to search for an opportunity to belong and contribute. There is no doubt that a charismatic individual such as Jim Jones met the psychological needs of his followers to the extent that they were prepared to drink poison and die for him.

And it happens here in the UK too. Chris Brain of the Nine O'Clock Service in Sheffield had the kind of charisma that demanded the sacrifice of a whole community. Fortunately, this did not include anyone's death. During the early 1990s he elicited huge financial gifts from followers to support his lifestyle. He persuaded young women in his congregation to serve him both in practical and sexual ways. Why? His followers, who included lawyers, doctors, professors, psychiatrists, theologians, football fans, churchmen and social workers, all felt that the Church of England needed revitalisation. They believed that Brain was a prophet who could do this and, what is more, they believed that he could change the world.

Those of us who are very susceptible to charismatics, and I am one of them, do feel empowered and energised by charismatic individuals. It is not just troubled folk who respond to charismatics. Dame Rennie Fritchie explained what she thought:

> 'Charisma is about being able to inspire people, to communicate in such a way that you inspire people to be able to feel the best they can feel, and to be able to do more than they could do before. It's more than just a feeling, it's about encouraging people so that it energises their behaviour and actions. I think charisma is about lifting people through inspiration to feel good, and be more alive and aware.'

Charisma depends on two things: the magnetism of the leader and the magnetisability of the followers.

So what is it that these charismatic individuals offer us?

The one thing a charismatic must have is a vision. No vision, no charisma. The needs of followers are in the main met by the mission and vision of the leader, and the importance of this vision is paramount. It is the vision that makes the leader different, that makes him or her stand out from the crowd. Nelson Mandela, the Ayatollah Khomeini and Adolf Hitler all promised profound change, which was all their followers wanted.

One of the most famous visions of our times is Martin Luther King. His 'I have a dream ...' speech, made at the 1963 march on Washington, is one of the most famous declarations of vision we have. It is interesting that his vision of social justice and equal rights in America meant different things to two very different sets of followers. For the American black population Martin Luther King offered the obvious – equal rights and justice. For his white followers, however, he reminded them of their guilt and offered them the opportunity for salvation by righting this appalling wrong. Visions can mean different things to different people.

Sometimes we may not like the visions, the differences that charismatics make:

'He just made a difference even if you didn't like the difference he made. There was never an occasion that he didn't make a difference.'
Les Williams talking about Robert Maxwell

Visions do not always have to be mega-visions. A charismatic's vision can be very personal, and not immediately associated with changing the world or major upheaval. They can be relatively simple visions which dictate how the individual concerned will behave and contribute to a particular goal or task. Many lesser-known charismatic people have a deep sense of personal vision and mission which enables them to contribute to a particular cause or charity, for example. Their appeal lies in their ability to inspire others to join them in this cause.

Tony Buzan put it this way:

'Charisma is the centre of an entire range of concepts. It implies that the individual possesses a number of characteristics. I think that the overriding characteristic is energy. Charisma requires an individual to have a vision, mission, goals and objectives of some sort. A charismatic person has the ability to transfer that vision with that energy to someone else who then receives it and, in a sense, becomes part of it.'

Wanted – followers for potentially charismatic leaders

The importance of followers must not be forgotten. Charismatic leaders and their followers are interdependent. Followers reinforce the leader's sense of mission and take the mission forward; immediate followers link the leader and the larger mass of potential followers. All the major religions of the world depend on the involvement and devotion of followers. We could argue that followership is as important as leadership!

'The people who are charismatic seem to me to have an ability to make people of whatever age and whatever background feel valued, and therefore those people are prepared to follow the charismatic person.'
Christine Dipple

The importance of oratory

Few well-known charismatics are poor speakers, and most are powerful orators. Martin Luther King was a particularly effective orator who used the old traditional skills of black Baptist preachers. However, it is worth noting that President Mandela and Ayatollah Khomeini are not affected by their lack of oratory. Years and years of imprisonment and exile deprived their followers of their voices but gave these two men an aura verging on martyrdom instead. If Nelson Mandela had not spent 27 years in prison, would he be viewed by the world as the saint-like figure he is seen as today?

Those I interviewed who had held or currently occupy positions of leadership all agreed that the ability to speak was one of the defining qualities of charisma. Peter Sharpe felt:

> 'It's the ability to make people listen to what you're saying. It means that your audience, the people with whom you are interacting, warm to what you're saying, listen to what you're saying and most importantly act upon what you're saying in the way that you would want them to act. You can't do that in a boring sort of way. You have to be charismatic to achieve that.'

There is a view that charisma today is a manufactured phenomenon and has more to do with stage management than spontaneous feeling. The Spice Girls must be the classic example here. They have a huge following and yet their image is entirely crafted to meet the expectations and aspirations of today's music market. The experts in this art are the media folk, PR consultants and spin doctors.

Personal appearance

Does one have to look like Venus or Adonis to be seen as charismatic? This leads right back again to the 'eye of the beholder', of course. Personal appearance may help, but it is a small part of the complex mixture of attributes. It is doubtful if Mahatma Gandhi, Mother Theresa, Martin Luther King, Adolf Hitler, Robert Maxwell or Mao Tse-Tung would have won a beauty contest anywhere in the world. However, for some, physical appearance is an important element of charismatic appeal. There is no doubt that the handsome John F Kennedy made considerable impact through his appearance. He personified the all-American war hero. He and his wife Jackie gave America its own 'royal family', with all the glitz, good looks and glamour of a Hollywood movie. The Kennedys had both the charisma of office and the visual charisma of appearance and lifestyle.

Some charismatics have a particularly piercing quality in their eyes. Charles Manson and Jim Jones are frequently quoted as having this particular quality. Broadcaster John Hendry met Colonel Gaddafi in the early 1970s and found him intensely charismatic. He particularly remembers the piercing intensity of his eyes, which seemed to seek out and hold the gaze of his audience.

Les Williams reflected on Robert Maxwell's charisma:

> 'It's about physical presence obviously, he was a big man.'

Are all charismatics the same?

No, they are not. What accounts for the differences between Mother Theresa and Hitler? Between Robert Maxwell and Heather Rabbatts, the CEO of the Borough of Lambeth? Research suggests that there are two types of charismatic personalities: *socialised* and *personalised* charismatics. Both types have many charismatic attributes in common, such as their confidence, vision, presentation, and ability to inspire their followers, but they differ markedly in a number of areas.

Socialised charismatic leaders share their goals and vision with their followers. These reflect the needs of both leader *and* follower.

Personalised charismatic leaders promote goals and vision which are internally generated – their own personal dream. This kind of charismatic leader has very clear personal motives which are then rationalised in terms of their followers' needs. Personalised leaders are not constrained by their followers' needs and aspirations, and are free to come up with very radical and novel solutions.

Socialised leaders are concerned to develop their followers as individuals whilst personalised leaders are only interested in their followers in so far as they assist them to achieve their own very personal goals. Socialised leaders appreciate and rely on intellectual stimulation from their followers as they develop and formulate their goals and ideas, whereas personalised leaders, once again, are only interested in their followers' views in so far as they assist in the achievement of their own goals.

The differences between socialised and personalised charismatic leaders may provide some of the answers as to why charisma can be so dangerous. It would appear that the individuals who we identify as dangerous, the ones that have misused their gifts – Hitler, Jim Jones, Charles Manson and Robert Maxwell, for example – were all personalised charismatics. The socialised charismatics are the good guys.

But what about the spiritual dimension of charisma? What happened to that?

Little emphasis is given to the spiritual aspect of charisma in academic research, even though the origin of the word implies a spiritual component – gift of the Spirit, gift of grace, recipient of divine inspiration. Mother Theresa was identified as charismatic by a large percentage of the questionnaire respondents and to these people the spiritual nature of charisma was very important. But we do not all agree. Sir John Harvey Jones and Dr Aubrey Wilson, for example, do not believe that charisma has a spiritual aspect. We are back to the eye of the beholder. A number of other people I interviewed believed strongly that their charisma had a spiritual dimension and was most certainly a gift. For example, Heather Rabbatts and

Dame Rennie Fritchie were quite clear that they have a spiritual dimension to their lives which is the basis for their lives and charismatic style. It may not be something that they shout about, but it is there and they are intensely aware of it.

'It has a spiritual quality and that's attached to belief. With belief there has to be truth. I think that is the spiritual quality'.

Nancy Wise

What do the academics say about charisma?

A trawl through the literature reveals considerable debate on the topic but few really dissenting views. Everyone who has examined the concept seems to believe that charisma exists and that it is associated with a number of behaviours and attributes. Most appear to think that it is a 'good thing', with potential pitfalls for the unwary. Most academics link charisma and leadership together, and there is a considerable body of work devoted to charismatic leadership which will be addressed in the next chapter.

There is no definitive definition but there is a general agreement about the constituent aspects of charisma. As we have seen, many of these were originally identified by Max Weber in the 1920s.

Weber's original five components of charisma are:

- An extraordinarily 'gifted' person
- A social crisis or desperate situation
- A set of ideas providing a radical solution to a crisis
- A set of followers attracted to the leader's exceptional powers – believing that he or she is linked to transcendent powers
- The validation of the exceptional powers by repeated success.

In addition charismatics have:

- Extremely high levels of self-confidence and dominance
- Strong convictions about the moral righteousness of their beliefs
- A strong need to have influence over others.

Their followers:

- Trust their charismatic's beliefs implicitly
- Offer willing and unquestioning obedience and affection
- Identify with and emulate the charismatic
- Have an intense emotional involvement with the vision
- Feel that they contribute to the success of the vision

- Achieve demanding goals
- Perceive the charismatic as successful
- See charisma as a powerful force for change
- Believe it occurs in all levels of society and in all cultures
- Believe it can have very important consequences and produce lasting effects, or
- It can dissipate with the death of the charismatic or a change in the environment.

For many people charisma has:

- An intensely spiritual dimension.

People with charisma have:

- A vision and mission
- A presence
- Confidence, energy and enthusiasm
- Self-determination
- Strong convictions
- A tendency to dominate
- A strong need to influence others
- An ability to feel intuitively what other people are feeling
- An outgoing nature
- Insight.

They sometimes have:

- Attractive physical features
- Hypnotic or arresting eyes
- A compelling, memorable voice
- A personal aura.

They are:

- Active, assertive and energetic
- Passionate.

It is obvious that these qualities themselves are *not* exclusive. Each one of us has some or all of these qualities. Charismatic individuals may have these qualities in greater intensity, but they are available to all of us. If we all have them in some measure then they are there for us to develop.

One more thing ... charismatics are 'revolutionaries'

Obviously, the gift of charisma is a very complex interaction of a number of qualities and attributes. In addition to all this, charismatic people achieve change. They are change masters. However, if this change is to last, the change has to be bedded in by setting up administrative systems which give others the opportunity to take on the power and authority of the charismatic person. This is called the 'routinisation of charisma'. This too implies that elements of the charismatic individual's behaviour can be adopted by others.

Sex

I had a long discussion with Robert Heller about charisma. He made the point that he thought that all the great charismatics were very sexually attractive. He quoted Napoleon, Hitler and Gandhi. Obviously I would like to have pursued this aspect with those I interviewed, but I didn't have the courage to ask them all what they felt about this suggestion. Was I sexually attracted to those I interviewed? That would be telling!

SO WHERE DOES ALL THIS LEAVE US?

Charisma gets a bad press today. When the gift is exploited and used badly it has dangerous and far-reaching consequences and the extreme charismatics have done us all a great disservice. The differences between socialised and personalised charismatic leaders may provide some of the answers as to why things can go wrong. It would appear that the individuals who we identify as dangerous, the ones that have misused their gifts, could all be described as personalised charismatics with internally generated visions. They were people who didn't interact with their followers to develop their vision and in the main were bent on achieving their own goals.

It is not surprising that a large number of people don't 'believe' in charisma, and many others think it is an inherently bad and destructive force. Fortunately, not all charismatic individuals are cast in this mould. Tony Benn told me that he did not believe in charisma and Robert Heller thinks that it is a very dangerous quality with no place in industry. I do not agree with either view. We owe a great debt to the great charismatics of the past – Elizabeth I, Martin Luther King, Churchill, and Disney, for example – and to those of today. The world would be a very dull place without them.

The message is quite clear: beware the personalised charismatic. Contain them. Develop and encourage the socialised charismatic. These are the people who can make a real and positive difference.

My survey said ...

Does all this theory really stand up though? I wanted to know what people generally thought about charisma – hence my survey. The results confirmed much of the summary above, but emphasised seven attributes above others – *confidence, vision, communication, bags of style, visibility, the ability to get things done, mystery and enigma.*

Those I interviewed agreed that these attributes made up a large measure of their own charisma. Hence, *The Keys of Charisma.* One thing more came out of my survey and that was that charismatics have a passion which drives everything that they do. Perhaps this is the *Key Ring*? (This may be pushing it a bit!)

I was very impressed by the views that came over in the survey. Charisma appears to be a prized quality, and one that people respect and admire. Consequently, it seemed important to me to see how we might all capitalise on our charismatic potential.

I have included a selection of the definitions of charisma made in the survey in the Appendix. Read them and see what you think.

Can we really learn to be charismatic?

I would not have written this book if I didn't think we could. I am not saying that we can all become like Lady Thatcher, Richard Branson or Nelson Mandela, but I am saying that we all have the seeds of charisma within us and we can understand and learn to develop our charismatic potential.

Jean-Marie Descarpentries agreed:

'I don't think charisma is a gift. You have to work at it!'

WHAT IS THE DIFFERENCE BETWEEN MANAGEMENT AND LEADERSHIP?
– views from the top

3

> 'There go my people, I must find out where they are going so that I can follow them and lead them.'

Lady Thatcher quoted a French politician as she chided an audience of top managers at Management Centre Europe's 1996 Top Management Forum in London. She was suggesting that too many leaders today were lost, lacking in direction. Her views on leadership include the absolute necessity for a sense of direction, the ability to make your mind up and do what you say you will.

The same conference included a number of business leaders from arround the world. Their recipes for successful leadership included those in direct opposition to Lady Thatcher's views.

> 'Leaders have to resist the pressure to give the answers.'

> ' People should be left to get on with managing or leading – on their own.'

> 'The job of the leader is to create the environment in which people are enabled to do what they enjoy doing.'

> 'It is about motivation, education, discipline, setting priorities, allocating limited resources, taking a long term view and being there when people need you.'

Mark McCormick of IMG likened good leadership to good parenting.
  There is no consensus there! There doesn't have to be. They are all right.

WHAT IS LEADERSHIP?

Views on leadership have been around for centuries. Sun Tzu, a general in the army of Ho Lu, King of Wu, wrote *The Art of War* in 490BC, Machiavelli expressed his thoughts in the sixteenth century, Mary Parker Follett, an American social scientist, explored the concept in the early part of the twentieth century, Field Marshal Montgomery identified his '10 Pillars of Leadership' after the Second World War, and General Colin Powell has been credited with creating 18 'priceless lessons' in the 1990s. And these are only a few of the students of leadership.

Leadership with magic dust

Then of course there are all the academic theories of leadership. First came the trait, behavioural and situational styles of leadership. Managerial grids, the path-goal theory, and transformational leadership entered our vocabularies. The academics realised that charismatic individuals appeared to reach quite spectacular levels of achievement and, consequently, charismatic leadership became a particular area of interest for many of them.

They found that charismatic leadership is leadership with magic dust. Charisma enhances leadership.

And is there a difference between leadership and management?

Managagement came into its own in the early part of the twentieth century when the French industrialist Henri Fayol described the processes involved in the effective running of his coal mining company. The techniques he used were revolutionary in their day and involved seeing management as a systematic activity. Fayol identified the processes we have come to associate with management – planning and control, motivation and reward, and communication. This rather simplistic view prevailed for many years until it became obvious through a number of research programes that management wasn't at all systematic and that there was a lot more to it. People began to distinguish between leadership and management.

Management became associated with complexity, while leadership is about change. Both management and leadership often involve the same activities – setting objectives, organising people to achieve these objectives and, finally, producing the desired outcomes. However, managers and leaders approach these activities in different ways. Management tackles them through planning and budgeting, organising and staffing, controlling and problem solving. It is a systematic, analytical approach. The leadership approach is one of synthesis. Two and two make five to give creative direction and achieve change for tomorrow. People are inspired and motivated to give their best.

Management and leadership are the opposite ends of the same continuum. It is important for all managers and leaders to develop the skills to move along this continuum either way to meet the demands of the situations in which they find themselves. There are times when a leader needs good systematic management skills and times when a manager must inspire people. We have to be able to do both, although most people will have a preference for a particular end of the continuum.

Management	Leadership

Organising	*Vision*
Implementing	*Process*
Complexity	*Change*
Today	*Future*

What is the best style of leadership?

There is no right answer. There is no one right way of leading anyone or anything. There is only the way that works for the leader and the led in a particular situation at a particular time within a particular set of circumstances.

Lady Thatcher quite clearly believes in a very up-front style of leadership – the Henry V style, made famous by both Lawrence Olivier and Kenneth Branagh. Who can forget 'Once more unto the breach, dear friends, once more'? The dictionary defines leadership as 'direction given by going in front', but 'in front' can mean many different things: in front with new ideas, or in front with the empowerment of others, for example.

Leadership seems to me to be about leaders feeling comfortable within themselves to such an extent that they are able to use their own personalities to create environments in which others can operate effectively. Success, in whatever way it is measured, comes about when there is congruence between the leaders and the led in terms of style.

Can leadership be learned?

I remember an eager young manager asking me what he had to do to be a better leader. He wanted me to give him a simple formula which he could immediately put into operation. Leadership isn't like that. Leadership is about individuals and the way they relate to their world. The best way to train to be a good leader is to concentrate on one's own personal development in the context of other people. Good leaders have an instinct for knowing what will work and why. Most leaders use their personalities to attract people to them, both personally and in terms of the kinds of environment they create. There is no one perfect model, but the one thing that we do know is that leaders with charisma can achieve out-of-the-ordinary results.

Leadership and charisma go hand in hand. We all have the potential for both charisma and leadership within us – and both are there to be developed.

FIVE EXPERTS ANSWER MY QUESTIONS AND COMMENT ON LEADERSHIP

Are leaders born or made?

' I probably haven't talked about passion. You have to enjoy leading. If you are standing there in a group of eight waiting for your turn to lead, and all the time you really want to lead rather than stand there, you want to be a leader. Instinctively I've always preferred to lead than to be led. I don't know why it is – bloody arrogance in a way because you always think you can do it better than the next bloke. Until you find out you can't you always believe you can. It's instinctive.'

Paul Lever

'Some people are born with some of the required characteristics of leadership. I think you can learn to lead well through a process of training. Quite clearly it is possible for people to be able to develop an understanding of the needs of their soldiers or the people who work for them, it's possible for them to see that they have got to identify with their needs and so on. But the best leaders are undoubtedly those who have a large element of the required talents in them at the very beginning.'

Sir John Acland

What are the qualities of good leaders?

'I think that leadership is getting people to do what needs to be done in the best possible way. I think the qualities for doing that are first, example and second, sympathy. Sympathy is the ability above all to understand the needs and interests of those for whom you are responsible down the line, and an ability to communicate in such a way that they will understand, so that they trust you and you then can get the best out of them.'

Sir John Acland

How would you describe the behaviour of effective leaders?

'The first thing that you're taught when you're shot at is to get down. Well, we were shot at for the first time so I got down and all my platoon got down. I put my head up a little bit to try and see where the bandits were and I remained there. After quite a long while a hand appeared on my shoulder – it was my platoon sergeant who had crawled up behind me and he said, "Come come sir, an officer can't remain lying down all the time, you have got to stand up and make a decision and get your men to stand up with you." Had it not been for him I might have been there for a very long time indeed! He displayed leadership; I didn't!'

Sir John Acland

'I believed and still believe that if you are responsible for leading an organisation, people have a right to know who you are, what you stand for and what sort of chap you are.

If you take the job of being the top man, you cannot then say, tough, I am going to stay at home and do it all by telephone calls. I also believe very strongly that leaders should lead by example. If you want an out-fit to behave in a particular way, you've got to behave that way. It is no good asking other people to do things that you don't personify. To that extent, I very consciously wanted my company to be much more achievement orientated and so I had to work like stink. I didn't feel I could ask them to do things if I was sloping off in a helicopter to play golf or something.'

Sir John Harvey Jones

'Credibility is important. The people in front of you must trust you when you say something. Trust involves the three "Bs" – belief, balls and brains. The other thing is success. You must be successful or you cannot remain a leader. Lastly, people need to understand that you serve them before serving yourself. When there is success in your company you praise the other guy and where there is a failure you take the blame.'

Jean-Marie Descarpentries

Is there a difference between management and leadership?

'I think there is a difference. You could be a very good manager and yet removed to some extent from your work force. Take a manager in the army; you could be a very good manager if you sat in an office. As the adjutant of the battalion responsible for all the details and admin-istrative arrangements, you can be an extremely efficient manager but without necessarily being a very good leader.

Leadership is a slightly different matter. one of the most important skills is the ability to communicate. You've got to speak a language which those to whom you're talking understand. People have to see that you are prepared to suffer the same discomforts and difficulties as they are. There are an awful lot of managers who at times may have been very good leaders and there are leaders who are also very good managers. The two are not necessarily separated.'

Sir John Acland

Do you have to be charismatic to be a leader?

'It helps because charismatic means you are a "selling man" and you sell your ideas as a leader. But you don't need to be a leader to be charismatic. A lot of leaders are not charismatic. Nixon was not charismatic and he was the President of the US.'

Jean-Marie Descarpentries

What are the problems of charismatic leadership?

'If you have a charismatic leader you lose all the other people who don't want to be followers – so that all the really talented people who don't want to be followers leave. I tend to get more women around me than men – (without being sexist) – because more women are prepared to be led, or work in that relationship. I don't work well with men, don't have much interest in working with men. I just think it is a "cock-fighting" thing.

Most people can't contribute to my vision either, unless they catch it before it is formulated – so I always tell everybody ... then is the time to say what they want because once the vision has gelled, it is all too late – I then go into producer sort of mode and start organising. I tend to get to the vision first – which gives me the high ground – and I have a skill which not all people who get to the vision first have got. I appear to be a good organiser and I am, because I have the characteristics of following through based on knowing where I am going.'

Gordon Wills

SUMMARY

- Leadership and management are two ends of the same continuum
- Theories of leadership:
  — Trait theories
  — Behavioural theories
  — Style theories
  — Situational leadership
- Charisma enhances leadership
- Management seen initially as – planning, control, motivating and communicating. Now seen as much more complex and unsystematic
- There is no one model of good leadership
- Effective leadership depends upon the leader, the led and the situation
- Charisma enhances leadership.

PART 2

The Keys of Charisma

HAVE YOU GOT 'CONFIDENCE IN CONFIDENCE ALONE' ...?

1. Tick those which describe you best
   (a) I have many good friends and acquaintances ☐
   (b) I prefer to have a few good friends only ☐
   (c) I am happiest in my own company ☐

2. Have you discussed or even thought about your own spirituality in the last year?
   (a) yes ☐
   (b) no ☐

3. Of the two extremes, do you prefer to be
   (a) one of a crowd? ☐
   (b) the odd 'man' out? ☐

4. How many major mistakes have you made in the last year?
   (a) none ☐
   (b) about five ☐
   (c) too many to count ☐

5. Do you know what your personal goals are?
   (a) yes ☐
   (b) no ☐

6. Do you know what your goals are?
   (a) yes ☐
   (b) no ☐

7. Which describes you best?
   (a) I 'serve time' at work ☐
   (b) I learn and gain experience at work ☐

8. How do you think other people might describe you? As
   (a) wallpaper ☐
   (b) a prickly bush ☐
   (c) an open fire ☐
   (d) a carpet ☐

9. I assess my own behaviour on a regular basis
   (a) yes ☐
   (b) no ☐

10. I   (a)   can   ☐
        (b)   cannot   ☐

demonstrate that I seek feedback on my behaviour from friends, colleagues and family on a regular basis.

11. As a *person*, are you
        (a)   very successful?   ☐
        (b)   successful?   ☐
        (c)   not successful?   ☐
        (d)   don't know?   ☐

Score

1. (a) 5	2. (a) 5	3. (a) 3	4. (a) −5	5. (a) 10	6. (a) 5
(b) 3	(b) −1	(b) 5	(b) 3	(b) 0	(b) 0
(c) 1			(c) 5		

7. (a) 0	8. (a) 1	9. (a) 5	10. (a) 5	11. (a) 5
(b) 5	(b) 3	(b) 0	(b) 0	(b) 4
	(c) 5			(c) 2
	(d) 1			(d) 0

Score ☐

Total available: 60 marks. If you scored:

- Over 55   Don't bother to read the Confidence Key – you have stacks of it!
- Between 40 and 55   You might pick up one or two tips.
- Between 30 and 40   Lots of room for improvement, but you are on the right track.
- Under 30   You have a lot of work to do to find yourself but do not be discouraged.

You can do it!

Key 1 THE CONFIDENCE KEY

WHAT *IS* CONFIDENCE?

The word comes from the Latin *confidere*, meaning 'to trust'. *The English Oxford Dictionary* defines the word as 'firm trust; assured expectation; self-reliance; boldness; impudence; trusting; fully assured; conviction'. This trust is in ourselves; we are all born with this quality. Initially, we have the potential to cope with every situation with confidence; as tiny children we have an in-built belief that we can take everything in our stride and deal with it successfully. This is how we learn. Daniel Goleman in his book *Emotional Intelligence* quotes a report by Dr T Berry Brazelton, an eminent Harvard paediatrician, in which confidence is listed as one of the ingredients of a child's crucial capacity to learn.

'*Confidence.* A sense of control and mastery of one's body, behaviour, and world; the child's sense that he is more likely than not to succeed at what he undertakes, and that adults will be helpful.'

'Confidence is a plant of slow growth in an aged bosom: youth is the season of credulity.'

William Pitt, 1770

We are all born with confidence, but the trick is to hang on to it. Hang on? Sadly, yes. Belief in ourselves can be easily knocked out of us instead of reinforced and nurtured. Parents are not always loving and supportive, adults are not always kind and reliable, teachers do not always have our best interests at heart, and our peers are often selfish and cruel. Events and circumstances can have a very negative impact on us. If this happens, we may have to work very hard to reclaim our confidence. And this is not easy.

Confidence comes from belief in oneself, from knowledge, experience and expertise. If we have confidence we can behave confidently. Benedict Allen felt his dreams helped:

'I am very tenacious, but, I strongly agree that we are born with confidence and it's a question of whether you can get through growing up and hang on to it. I think I've circumvented the system because I had such strong dreams.'

JOURNEY TO THE CENTRE OF THE ONION

Each one of us is like an onion, layer upon layer. Some of these layers are easily visible to others, some are not. At first, we may not even be able to see some of the deepest layers ourselves.

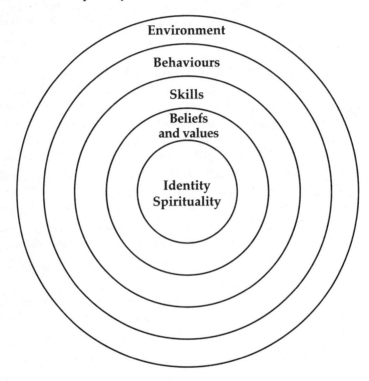

Journey to the centre of the onion

The outer layer represents the environment that we create for ourselves – home, place of work, car or whatever. We 'tell' people things about ourselves through the kind of house we live in, how we arrange our office or desk, the clothes we wear, what pictures we have around us, what kind of car we drive – or not, as the case may be. In the very materialistic world in which we live, this layer provides information about how we perceive our status in life. (We would of course be better advised to heed the warning 'Don't judge a book by its cover'!)

Underneath this comes a layer which is described by our behaviour. The way we interact with our family, colleagues, peers, acquaintances and friends gives away yet more personal information. Bully, caring, considerate, short-tempered, ambitious, self-seeking, loyal, reliable: these are the kinds of words people use to describe the way we behave towards others.

We give away information about this layer as soon as we open our mouths! The third layer is less easily seen by others and consists of the skills we have. These have to be demonstrated or at least talked about, because it is not automatically obvious that an individual may have specific technical or work skills, or be a talented author, cook, counsellor or linguist, for example.

Buried a little deeper comes our values and beliefs layer. These can be secret even from ourselves! There are many occasions when we hear people say that they have just found out what is important to them – usually after a traumatic event or experience such as a heart attack or a serious accident. People learn what they really value in their lives – themselves, their family and friends, perhaps.

Right in the centre, buried so deep that many of us have to work hard to find it, lies our real self. This is our very centre, where our notions of 'I', 'me' and 'my' stem from. Real confidence stems from this centre core and there are many who would say that our lives are a search for that centre core. Once we realise that 'I' can change all the other layers if 'I' so choose, we have personal confidence. 'I' is in charge. When we get it right, all the other layers of our being reflect the nature of our core. If they don't and are out of alignment then we have problems. Real confidence comes from knowing that we are behaving in a way which reflects our inner being. However, we all have to journey to get there! Dame Rennie Fritchie has her own way of describing this:

> 'The only thing I haven't talked about is the inner bit, which is how you keep yourself grounded. Centred in my chest I think I have something like a spirit level; a spirit level has a tube of glass and a bubble centred between two lines when things are on the level. Being a grown up human being is about knowing where *you* draw the line and how you centre the bubble. When you're a child your parents tell you the rules of life and what you should and shouldn't do. These are their lines or society's lines. Then as you get older you test these and redraw them. For me the confidence comes from consistently working towards a balance. What it's OK for me to do and what it's not OK for me to do, and measuring my self and my growth by being consistent and conscious of my own actions in line with my beliefs.'

The core of confidence is self-esteem and what we believe about ourselves – the believing and knowing oneself. Everything else follows from this.

How is a louse relevant?

We receive feedback on behaviour from those around us, from our work, and from our achievements. This helps us to build up a picture of ourselves. If we deal with the information honestly we are able to feel good about our successes – and to identify areas in which we would like to make progress.

If we are not used to dealing with feedback in this way, admitting that we are good at things can be very uncomfortable. For some it will feel 'sinful', particularly if they have had a very religious upbringing. Women tend to find this more difficult than the majority of men. Americans appear to find it easier than many of the more reserved Europeans.

As to the louse?

> O wad some Pow'r the giftie gie us
> To see oursels as other see us!
> It wad frae mony a blunder free us,
> And foolish notion.
>
> *Robert Burns, 'To a Louse'*

Belief in oneself

Often we are not prepared to believe the evidence of our own ears and eyes. Although we may receive positive feedback on our performance from family, friends and work colleagues, many of us tend strongly towards self-doubt. We *refuse* to believe the evidence in front of us. And then, to make it worse, we project these negative views of ourselves on to others and think that that is what they think of us! We have to 'get real' and be honest with ourselves. When we are appraising anyone else, we give them full credit for their achievements – and so it has to be when we are assessing ourselves.

Negative thinking has to stop. In his *Book of Genius*, Tony Buzan says 'positive self-talk directed to the accomplishment of goals must take its place. We all self-talk and psychological researches have shown that as much as 90 per cent tends to be negative – for instance ... "I'd never be able to do that".'

Even charismatic individuals have their moments of self-doubt too. None of my interviewees gave me the impression that they were always right, always knew the answers and always knew where they were going. Here's Fred Dibnah:

> 'I often feel a failure, I feel sometimes as though everything is going wrong for me, when things don't go quite right. Like this old chimney, in all my career we've only had three of them. Why haven't I been asked to deal with more? I suppose in a way it's like being in a race and coming second.'

BUILDING SELF-ESTEEM

The visioning technique

The majority of athletes use visioning techniques to help them achieve their goals. They run through the event in question, imagining the actual physical experience of the competition and finally 'feeling' what it would be like to win, experiencing the roar of the crowd and the excitement of the medal ceremony. This programmes the brain positively, maximising the potential for success.

In his book *In Pursuit of Sporting Excellence*, David Hemery describes a series of interviews with achievers from all walks of life:

> 'Visualisation was considered to be the most important aspect these achievers had in common. They sensed with the greatest possible clarity the successful performance of their ambition. At times this involved using all their senses; they would imagine the sound, sight, touch, taste and smell of the coming challenge and its successful outcome ... It is important that the action is as close to perfection as one's mind can conceive.'

Hemery believes that this approach has a number of advantages. It allows the individual to have 'been there' before the event and, therefore, some of the element of fear of the unknown can be resolved – and, perhaps most importantly, the individual is convincing him or herself that successful action is possible. This means that one is working on an improved self-image which can increase one's self-confidence, and confidence is all important in performing well under stressful conditions. He believes that visualisation is the mind's way of rehearsing personal control of successful actions.

I know that this technique works for me. I had frightened myself before a presentation and wasn't at all confident that all would go well. I decided to take a little of my own medicine and try out the visioning technique. I sat down quietly and imagined the looks on people's faces as they listened to me. I imagined the applause at the end and people coming up to me asking me questions. I felt the glow when people said how much they had valued and enjoyed my presentation. I started my presentation knowing that it would be successful. It was.

Achievement banks

Another way of building self-esteem is to create a visual bank for achievements. Make notes on successes, file appreciative letters, put in photographs of events in which you have participated which reflect success, and photographs of material things which reflect the success you have achieved. Update your CV on a regular basis and include it in your 'bank'. It is so easy to forget, to disregard the evidence of the past unless we consciously record it and give it value. Sports people are fortunate in that they are given very visible trophies to mark their successes. Those of us in other walks of life need to surround ourselves with reminders of our achievements in other ways. I have a small porcelain bell given to me by a Czech lady on one of my courses. She said that I had rung a bell of freedom for her. This is a very special bell for me.

Dame Rennie Fritchie keeps a file of 'nice letters'. When she feels depressed and things are tough she looks at the file to remind herself that she is an achiever and is very much appreciated. When she decided to stand down as Chair of the Regional NHS executive, South and West, in March 1996 she received 85 letters of appreciation. All of these letters went into her file!

We can all find examples of other people's appreciation of our contribution. Remember and value these. They can help and support us in the bad times.

Fear of failure or learning from mistakes?

'Half the failures in life arise from pulling in one's horse as he is leaping.'

Julius Hare 1795–1855 and Augustus Hare 1792–1834

Having a go, not being frightened to get it wrong or to be refused, together with the ability to continuously learn from mistakes – these are characteristics of truly charismatic individuals.

A profoundly deaf young girl announces that she is going to be a musician! There must be a number of medical men in Glasgow whose understanding of the human spirit has undergone a radical review. Evelyn Glennie confounded everyone but herself.

The much quoted failure Abraham Lincoln failed in business at 22, was initially defeated for the Legislature at 23, failed in business again, had a nervous breakdown at 27, was defeated for Speaker at 29, defeated for Elector at 31, defeated for Congress at 34, was elected to Congress again, then defeated at 39, defeated for Senate at 46, defeated for Vice-President at 47, defeated for Senate again at 49, but then elected as President of the United States in 1860 at the age of 51.

Thomas Watson Snr, the founder and first President of IBM, is quoted as saying:

'Double your rate of failure … Failure is a teacher – a harsh one perhaps, but the best. That's what I have to do when an idea backfires or sales programme fails. You've got to put failure to work for you … You can be discouraged by failure or you can learn from it. So go ahead and make mistakes. Make all you can. Because that's where you will find success. On the far side of failure.'

Of course it can be humiliating to fail, but failure must be put into perspective. What is the worst that can happen if things do not work out as planned? In January 1997 Richard Branson gathered the world's press together to witness the launch of his attempt to circumnavigate the world in a hot air balloon. The journey should have taken 18 days. He landed within 24 hours! Humiliated? Not a bit of it. He is determined to try again.

I know two managers who are terrified of making mistakes. They believe that they will get the sack if they do. My view is that they will probably get the sack if they don't. They aren't learning much and consequently add less and less value to the organisations. Managers face very few situations in which the answer is a firing squad! As Ross Perot said, 'Failures are like skinned knees ... painful but superficial, they heal quickly.' Evelyn Glennie put it like this:

> 'I do feel confident but I don't mean that in a complacent manner. It's more the confidence to experiment really and not being too frightened to pick myself up should something go wrong, which can so often happen.

Failing in one of the outer layers of the onion does not damage the inner core, providing we have a deep knowledge of ourselves. Failing in a particular endeavour does not mean that we are any the less a person for that failure. Understanding that means that we have achieved real confidence. We have the confidence to put it right, to do it again, to do something different, or to walk away, learning from the experience. It is always sad to read about people who have committed suicide because they have failed in their business ventures, relationships, examinations or whatever. They have got stuck in a particular layer. Sadly, they have not realised that this particular failure is part of their life's experience that they can learn from – and then move on to other things.

SERVING TIME

What is the difference between experience and expertise?

There is a great deal of difference between experiencing something and spending time at something. Experiencing something means recognising in ourselves the feelings generated by the events in question, and recognising that one has been affected by knowledge or events; it means that we have *learned* from the event or knowledge and that, as a consequence, our behaviour will be different in the future. Spending time at something means exactly that. How many managers just serve time in their organisations rather than gaining experience? It is quite possible to spend just one year in a role and to have more experience than someone else who has spent ten years in the same role if the first person learns and responds, but the latter just marks time. It is the learning and responding that maintains and enhances personal confidence. Where confidence is lacking, experience can create confidence within an individual. For Evelyn Glennie,

> 'Experience means I feel more confident towards the music business too. Dealing with more repertoire and so on means I've less time to think about the actual mechanics of playing. I can no longer spend eight hours running up and down the scale and things like that. Having the confidence to go five, six, seven days without touching an instrument and then immediately play and switch on. That kind of confidence is quite important.'

Becoming an expert is a real confidence-booster. Most of us would like to be an expert, someone who has special knowledge or skill in a particular area. The acquisition of experience and expertise does not happen overnight. Both require commitment and dedication: a commitment to learning from the events and happenings of both our personal and professional lives, and a formal commitment to developing a better-than-average knowledge or skill in something. Again, this requires the ability to learn and a lot of hard work. It does not just happen.

Experts know more about something than anyone else, apart from another expert. How does one become an expert? First, by deciding that you want to become an expert! Then, by devoting a great deal of time and energy to learning more, in more detail than anyone else, and then using this knowledge and expertise in appropriate situations. Fred Dibnah is an expert steam engineer and steeplejack. He has spent his whole life working in these two areas. Restoring his steam-roller took 14 years and he has done most of the work himself. He has only needed help in areas where he hasn't the appropriate facilities. However, he totally understands the processes that he is buying in. Meeting him, there is no doubt that he is in love with his work. There is no dividing line between his work and the rest of his life and his passion for steam and chimneys is obvious. He has made himself an expert. He has had no engineering training and became an expert through continuous learning, application and simple trial and error, learning from his mistakes as he went along.

For Sir John Acland, confidence is all about training.

> 'Confidence comes from training and if someone hasn't got confidence in themselves to do their job properly they are bound to fail. Expertise is training, experience speaks for itself, belief in oneself comes from the training you have and the belief that you have the knowledge to do your job.'

Evelyn Glennie is an expert in percussion. She did have formal training at the Royal Academy of Music in London and in Japan on a Munster Scholarship, but for many years now has planned her own learning. She travels the world experimenting and learning at every opportunity. There is no doubt about it that she also is in love with her work. Sir John Harvey Jones is an expert in a whole range of areas, particularly those of leadership and trouble-shooting. How has he got there? Continuous learning; reading, talking, discussion and doing. He told me that he has probably read everything of substance written on leadership. How many other consultants can say that?

All three of them have four things in common:

- Curiosity and a real desire to *know*
- An immense appetite for learning and new ideas
- The courage to take risks
- They are in love with what they do and make no apology for this.

It goes without saying that experience may make you an expert, but you can be an expert in something and yet lack experience.

'If you have a wonderful vision then you will have extraordinary energy about it. You will also find that the charismatic individual is exceptionally knowledgeable which again influences the mind of the observer, the listener. Observers know that charismatic individuals, have, for whatever reason, devoted a lot of time to accumulate data which means they must have energy and focus – we love to follow people with energy and focus. Look at any sporting event, what raises the entire stadium to its feet? The person with the most energy and focus at that time. The one who scores the goal, who wins by a knock-out in the first round, whatever it is, it is vision, energy, focus, knowledge of the area.'

Tony Buzan

BEHAVING CONFIDENTLY

'No one can make you feel inferior without your own consent.'
Eleanor Roosevelt

An immediate reaction might be to disagree. Of *course* people can diminish our confidence, through their aggressive behaviour, their criticism, their general disregard for us: in fact by any number of things that they might do. They can do this just by being good at something! It is easy to move the responsibility for our loss of confidence to other people. It's their fault. The problem with this is that it leaves us with no power at all. We have given it away to the other person, so that unless other people change the way they behave towards us we cannot do what we want to. We become totally dependent on the whims and fancies of others. It is only when we learn to put distance between other people and ourselves, when we learn to respect ourselves, when we learn to separate ourselves from our own behaviour that we have any hope of regaining control over our own situation. We have to take responsibility for ourselves. It is important to recognise any weaknesses and shortcomings, whether personal or professional and then address them.

We need to take the same responsible attitude when confronting our fears. It is unusual not to have been confronted by fear of failure, fear of isolation and rejection, loss of identity and lack of competence. We have all been faced with these, and charismatic people are no exception. What matters is whether we face up to our fears or not. And having faced up to them, whether we have thought them through and identified the component elements, and then taken action to resolve these issues. This may mean learning new technical skills, improving interpersonal skills, or attempting the very difficult task of changing the way we look at things. It may mean changing our behaviour and ways of doing things, behaviours which may have been in place for decades.

We may need help, and even acknowledging this requires courage. We need courage to *recognise* the need and courage to *take action*, courage to ask colleagues for help and feedback, to attend an interpersonal skills course, to update professional training, or to admit we were wrong and take on new ideas. It takes particular courage to seek help from a counsellor or psychotherapist. A number of the charismatic people interviewed for this book have seen a counsellor or psychotherapist for substantial lengths of time and all say they benefited considerably from the experience. Sadly, seeking such help is frequently ridiculed in the media. More courage is required to overcome such prejudices!

Sometimes we need encouragement to be courageous. Sir John Acland described a situation in which encouragement was required to spark off immense courage:

'A very young officer with his platoon woke up in the cold clear light of dawn in the bush and they saw 300 guerrillas in their arrowhead attack formation coming in with their weapons on their hips. The young officer said to his sergeant major, "What the hell do we do now, only ten men here?" The advice he got from the sergeant major, which he took was, "You put down your weapon and you walk forward with your hand outstretched like a proper British gentleman." So he got up and he walked slowly towards the guerrillas. Finally he came to the leading man and he took his hand off the grip of his weapon and offered it. The leader took it and the ice was broken. Had he stayed where he was, or had he ordered his men to open fire on the guerrillas, not only would they probably all have been killed, but the whole cease-fire would have collapsed and there would then have been no election in Rhodesia.'

Recognising and acknowledging our own ability is very important when it comes to building on our confidence. Some of us are loath to admit to our attributes and expertise, normally because we have been taught that to do so is immodest. Acknowledging personal ability does not imply denigration of others' ability – it means recognising God-given gifts, if you are a believer, or natural ability if you are not. Who can forget Eric Liddell's recognition of his athletic gift in the film *Chariots of Fire*. Daley Thompson and Evelyn Glennie are good examples of individuals who know they have extraordinary abilities.

Daley Thompson won two Olympic gold medals in the decathlon, in 1980 and 1984.

'It never occurred to me that I would ever lose anything.'

'There were just days when I just couldn't throw, and things just weren't happening. Then you just cut your losses and hope that it is going to be better next day. I always knew it would be.'

Will Carling and Robert Heller in their book *The Way to Win* include an excellent chapter which describes Daley Thompson's approach to winning. This is best described as self-belief underpinned by consistent training, and setting stretching but personally achievable goals. In addition, Thompson believes that it is important to be realistic about one's level of ability. He says in *The Way to Win* 'If you are honest, and achieve that level – the best of your ability – you should never lose confidence'.

Heather Rabbatts knew that she could make something of her life, even though on the surface she didn't appear to have much academic ability. Talking to her, I felt that she was well aware of other gifts – particularly the gift of charisma. Her confidence appears to come from a very strong belief in herself.

'I do think charisma is a gift but I feel I have been enormously lucky and privileged. I failed my 11 plus and all sorts of doors looked closed for me. But I "got out" and have become successful, whatever that word might mean. Now I feel I ought to give something back. I'm not using the word "debt" because I don't feel burdened by it but I want to give something back, and therefore I'm driven in that particular way.'

I asked Barry John where his confidence came from. His response – 'ability'.

'A man going nowhere usually gets there.'

Anon

Obvious really. We all need to know what we are trying to do. If we don't, then it is unlikely that we will achieve much! Setting goals is important. These goals can be big and very obvious to others, or they can be simple, understated and private. Personal mission statements are one way of identifying private goals, and job targets and appraisal action plans illustrate professional goals.

I remember being much influenced by an article written by Dr Beverly Potter of Stanford University in 1985, in which she suggested that in personal career planning we need to be very careful when setting goals. It is easy to 'miss' our target and fail to achieve a specific goal, such as becoming Managing Director, or Head of the Department, through no real fault of our own. Other people can so easily get in the way and, no matter what we do, we *cannot* achieve the goal! Built in failure. She recommends that we aim to *capture territory* instead – that is, to achieve mastery in a particular *area*. This might be in the general management arena, it might be in marketing or sales, production or IT – whatever. If we capture territory we have so many more options open to us. The goal becomes less specific. The target area is much bigger and consequently we have increased our chances of achieving, rather than being undermined by failures to achieve unrealistic goals.

Self-confidence is about *who* you are, not what you look like

Sometimes confidence means daring to be different, to stand out from the crowd. It means being totally confident going to a 'white tie do' without the white tie. It means being able to wear a pullover when everyone else around you is dressed in the regulation suit. It means being able to be large when small and skinny is trumpeted as the ideal. Nelson Mandela was not asked to go home and put his white tie on when he dined with the Queen, Richard Branson must have more pullovers than Val Doonican, and Dawn French does not spend her life on a diet. Fair enough – one might say that no one would dare to send Nelson Mandela home to change. In one sense, perhaps, someone did, and he spent 27 years in prison because he would not change. Richard Branson was pilloried in the press, particularly by Lord King, then of British Airways, because he did not wear a suit. Dawn French has refused to conform to the majority idea of what shape she ought to be. All three know who they are and are not concerned with what others think about them. All three have courage and bags of self-confidence. I learnt this lesson myself, courtesy of British Airways. In the last year they have mislaid my luggage twice and I have had to run seminars in my rather scruffy travelling clothes. On both occasions no one minded. 'It's you we came to see, not your clothes', replied an engineer in response to my apology.

The relevance of sliced bread

Self-confidence needs to be nurtured. Self-confident people are rarely lazy. They work very hard at maintaining and enhancing their self-confidence. Rather like swans, they glide effortlessly by while paddling furiously underwater. Most truly self-confident people pay a great deal of attention to detail. Second best will not do for them.

If you do not think you are the 'best thing since sliced bread' no one else will!

> 'I would love to meet Sir John Harvey Jones, he's got that twinkle and assurance and approachability or something or another that I just find very intriguing.'
>
> *Evelyn Glennie*

> 'I learned to have confidence in myself. I consciously learnt to work on my self-image after my divorce. I was in a terrible state and all of that kind of thing. I went to counselling and it worked for me. If I'm feeling bad I would go back. I think I learnt from the experience of being very healthy to having cancer how valued I was by people, by my friends, my family and so on and that was good, it was very nurturing. So having confidence in yourself is the thing, knowing your subject and understanding that on the whole people want to give you a fair wind, they don't want to put you down. I've learned about the media as well. They may want to put politicians down but on the whole John Humphrys wants me to say my piece in an effective way, and so does Jimmy Young. That builds my confidence too.'
>
> *Baroness Pitkeathley*

PAUPERS AND PRINCES

Jeffrey Archer's explanation as to why there are more 'paupers in the world than princes' has some bearing on this discussion. It goes something like this:

If you have talent and energy you can become a king;
If you have no talent but you have energy you can become a prince;
If you have talent but no energy you will be a pauper.

Energy and motivation are the secrets of success. I did not meet any charismatic individuals who lacked energy and personal motivation. Their motivation came from within and none of them sat around waiting for someone else to 'motivate' them. Others can create environments which support an individual's motivation, but no one can motivate another person. They can frighten, bully, encourage or support, but the motivation itself, that inner drive, has to come from within. Many of us lack energy – that is why there are more paupers than princes and kings. Energy and motivation enable us to overcome realistic hurdles. There is a view that we have more mediocre individuals in the public arena than talented ones. Many of the talented ones do not have the energy and drive required to get to the top or into the spotlight. Pity!

But ... the really special people achieve even where it is not realistic to expect they can! Anyone who says that the sky is the limit is short on imagination. Talent alone did not ensure Evelyn Glennie's success. Without her personal motivation, determination and drive we would not have heard of her! It's energy and personal motivation that enable people to train consistently, to go to evening classes, to study when others are playing, to make sacrifices to pay for their own training and development, to push themselves hard. It is energy and determination which will not take 'no' for an answer! Confidence is fuelled by success, by energy and enthusiasm. Energy comes in many guises. Energy makes things happen. Energy comes from the centre of the onion.

SUMMARY

- 'Confidence is a sense of mastery of one's body, behaviour and world.'
  Dr T Berry Brazelton

- We are made up of five layers which must all be in alignment:
  — environment
  — behaviour
  — skills
  — values and beliefs
  — 'I' – self
- We must see ourselves as others see us
- Making mistakes is fine as long as one learns from the experience
- There is a real difference between serving time and gaining experience
- A sense of personal ability is important

- 'A man going nowhere usually gets there'
- Self-confidence is about who you are, not what you look like
- Courage is an integral part of confidence.

Action points

- Accept and believe honest feedback – positive or negative
- 'See' success through visioning
- Create visual achievement banks
- Find the courage to 'have a go'
- Learn from mistakes
- Gain experience *and* expertise
- Recognise personal capabilities and limitations
- Set achievable goals but strive to exceed these
- Behave confidently
- Above all, *know who you are.*

The secret ingredients are **Energy, Motivation and Drive**.

DO YOU USE YOUR VISIONARY POWERS?

1. Do you have a good idea of the kinds of thing that you want to have achieved in your life?
    (a) yes ☐
    (b) no ☐

2. Do you have a good idea of the kind of person you want to be?
    (a) yes ☐
    (b) no ☐

3. Do you want to get up in the morning?
    (a) sometimes ☐
    (b) never ☐
    (c) always ☐

4. There are
    (a) too many ☐
    (b) not enough ☐
    (c) just enough hours in the day? ☐

5. Could you list the five most important values in your life?
    (a) I've thought about it but would need time to get them just right ☐
    (b) quickly and easily ☐
    (c) no ☐

6. Do you enjoy dreaming?
    (a) no ☐
    (b) yes, but I wouldn't admit this ☐
    (c) yes, and people know this about me ☐

7. Do you think dreaming is important?
    (a) no ☐
    (b) yes ☐

8. Have you been able to turn any of your dreams into reality?
    (a) no ☐
    (b) yes ☐

9. Have you ever told your manager that you need time to think and dream?
    (a) certainly not! ☐
    (b) yes ☐

10. If you hear a colleague arguing passionately for something you agree with, do you
    (a) feel embarrassed for her ☐
    (b) admire her but keep quiet ☐
    (c) join in ☐

11. Which kinds of people do you admire most?
    (a) logical and rational ☐
    (b) creative and unorthodox ☐
    (c) neither one nor the other ☐
    (d) both ☐

Score

1. (a) 5	2. (a) 5	3. (a) 3	4. (a) 0	5. (a) 3	6. (a) 0
(b) 2	(b) 0	(b) –1	(b) 5	(b) 5	(b) 3
		(c) 5	(c) 3	(c) 0	(c) 5
7. (a) –1	8. (a) 0	9. (a) 0	10. (a) –5	11. (a) 4	
(b) 5	(b) 5	(b) 10	(b) 0	(b) 5	
			(c) 5	(c) 0	
				(d) 3	

Score ☐

Total available: 60 marks. If you scored:

➤ Over 55   You are a person of vision, direction and passion.
➤ Between 40 and 55   You might pick up one or two tips but your sense of vision is developing.
➤ Between 30 and 40   Lots of work to do here to realise your potential and achieve direction.
➤ Under 30   Find someone you admire for their purpose in life and ask them to help you explore your own buried dreams.

Key 2 THE VISION KEY

'I was inspired by people like Walter Raleigh and I had a sort of dream. I was drawn by very different things; I was incredibly inquisitive, as I still am, but I was also driven by a sort of romanticism – I wanted to be an explorer. I'm one of those lucky people who've actually managed to fulfil their dream and I do exactly what I have always wanted to do. At first I didn't really have the courage to think I could do it but it has happened for me.'

Benedict Allen

Some people have always known what they wanted to do with their lives. It might be working with horses, flying aeroplanes, teaching, or even becoming an explorer. These are the lucky folk! Many of the rest of us did not have a very clear idea of our future when we were at school, never mind now. We might have vague notions, but few for which we have a real passion. One of the reasons why many of us do not have a vision of what we want to do in life is that we think a 'vision' should be rather grandiose, something that is very clear, like becoming an MP, or even Prime Minister. Many of us just don't see ourselves with goals like this. But vision does not have to be defined in this way. Benedict Allen described his thought processes like this:

'Lots of times I thought that I could never *really* become an explorer. I thought 'oh well – I'll have to settle down to a sensible job' and so I read environmental sciences which was perfect. Then I thought that maybe I should be a landscape architect, or a geologist, or even an ecologist. I was trying to do what everyone else does really – fit into society's mould, quite naturally because I am part of our society. But I gave it one go and I thought I'd just be an explorer on one journey. That sparked it off and I realised that I could create a niche for myself.'

Fred Dibnah said that he is now living his dream but he got there slowly:

'Well all of this here is a dream really. It's strange when I found that steam engine that's in that shed. I never envisaged it would end up doing what it does.'

> 'Yes, people do tell me about their dreams; they are often middle aged people, or younger people who say things like "I've always kind of thought about doing something like you but I didn't have the chance" or "I didn't have the money" or something. They want to be a part of what I'm doing.'
>
> *Evelyn Glennie*

> 'I always knew that I wanted to teach and I began at about six or seven – I taught my dolls. Then I started teaching at Sunday School when I was about 15. I had quite a number of years behind me before I ever got into a classroom!'
>
> *Cynthia Homer*

VISIONS OFTEN GENERATE MISSIONS

Vision and mission are words that are frequently, but erroneously, used interchangeably. Defining the difference between vision and mission is important, particularly for those of us working in organisations with mission and vision statements. The words themselves come from two different routes. Vision comes from the Latin 'visio', to see, and mission from 'mittere', to send. A *vision* involves seeing something that does not currently exist, having imaginative insight. Consequently a vision may be entirely fanciful, but is not necessarily so. A *mission*, on the other hand, is much more concrete in nature. *It requires that something is done.* Missionaries have very specific tasks. They are sent out to 'do' something, normally to convert others to a particular way of thinking. A mission statement is a description of what a company intends to do.

All charismatic people have vision and for many, their vision leads into their mission. They continue to have vision throughout their lives because vision is in the mind and continues to change and develop as it responds to the individual's increased experience, knowledge and understanding of the world. Their missions, or the tasks they set themselves, may be completed and new missions identified. John Kennedy's mission to land a man on the moon before the end of the decade was a very clear statement of mission. This mission came out of the American vision of space travel for the future. Now the American vision of space is not as clear as it was. They appear less imaginative about space travel for the future and the mission in space is less obvious. The emphasis appears to be on machines in space, not human beings, which have a lower profile and less impact. However, the recent Soujowner mission to Mars has rekindled some of the former enthusiasm and scientists are now working on their visions of humans travelling further in space, with all that implies. My interviewees had lots to say about vision. Sometimes their vision, sometimes other people's visions. Here are some of the thoughts which particularly impressed me:

'I had the pleasure of meeting Josephine Baker, through my father; she was totally charismatic but she also had a vision – do you remember the rainbow children? She wanted to bring world peace – she hoped that racism would disappear. She tried to do something about it but sadly she died a disappointed woman. But she had a vision.'

Pia Helena Ormerod

'When I got involved in industrial relations, I had a real vision. I passionately believed that there was a role for the trade union movement and that the "them and us" situation had to be reversed ...'

Paul Lever

'When I decided on my vision, things changed. That vision was born out of pain and frustration and delight. I didn't know how to learn. No one else that I knew had been taught how to learn, how to use their amazing physical and mental skills. My goal in life became to help make the planet Earth mentally literate in which everyone understood the hardware and software of their brain and of their bodies.'

Tony Buzan

'If you're a rudderless ship then I don't see again how you can be successful. So if I'd taken over as the Chief Constable of Hertfordshire and said, "OK in the next 24 hours we will deliver a service" I don't think it would have worked. I had to say, 'Right, in the next ten years my vision for us is this ... our mission is ... we must achieve ... and so on. My vision is to create a safer Hertfordshire and to build an organisation that's confident in it's own ability and feels like a winner.'

Peter Sharpe

'I link strategy and vision together. As far as planning goals, aims, that kind of thing, that's always been part of my life which is quite handy. I think ten years ahead, which is very reasonable considering that a musician's diary can be booked five years ahead. I've got to think how I might be at the age of 40 or 50. Am I going to be able to do this or that or will I want to do something else?'

Evelyn Glennie

'Margaret Thatcher had one of the clearest visions of any European politician this century. Her vision was so clear in her mind that everything that she did related to her vision. Her gigantic knowledge of history was awesome. MPs in the House of Commons were afraid of her because her vision was so clear and her knowledge so complete that they felt powerless. Not because of any superiority of intellect, but because they knew that if they tangled with this giant vision, it would wipe them out, rather like some mythological god, even if it were wrong. Vision doesn't necessarily have to be right but if it is strong and well supported it will tend to be victorious over those who don't have a strong vision.'

Tony Buzan

'If you don't have vision then you cannot be a leader and if you have vision without ambition – you are a prophet – not a leader. You need ambitious vision. These two things are extreme and rather contradictory. If you have only one of the two, it's not enough. Vision without short-term ambition will show no results.'

Jean-Marie Descarpentries

Tony Buzan reminded me of Coca-Cola's vision which everyone in Coca-Cola shares – to put a can of Coca-Cola within arms' reach of every person on the planet. In 1969 I led a party of young Tanzanian students on a folk singing tour around the country; at one point our mini-bus got stuck in the mud in the Serengeti and one of my students and I walked for several hours into the bush in the hot sun to find help. We arrived at a Masai boma and were shown into a dark mud hut by very friendly villagers. There, standing proudly on a wooden plank, supported by mud bricks were three cans of Coca-Cola – hundreds of miles from the nearest town! Coca-Cola were pretty good at making their vision a reality 27 years ago.

Hurray for our right brains!

Visions are very personal things. Organisations do not have visions. People have visions, which become the organisation's shared vision. The right cortex, which is responsible for idealistic and intuitive thinking (imagination, emotion, conceptualisation and synthesis) must have its contribution recognised as equally important as the activities of the left cortex, which is responsible for realistic and logical thinking (quantitative, critical, structured and controlled thinking). We often refer to this in short-hand as right brain and left brain rather than using the more accurate term 'cortex'.

This means accepting that there are different styles of thinking and that a different style of thinking is not wrong, just different. People who are predominantly left-brain thinkers may have to make conscious efforts to allow their right brain to take a greater part in their lives. Ned Herrmann's work in this area, which is very well set out in his book, *The Whole Brain Business Book*, is a superb contribution to our understanding of our own potential. In our modern competitive and technological world we tend to value left-brain activities far more than those of the right brain. However, the demands of current discontinuous change have prompted us to use the potential of our right brains to address the major issues of the future. New thinking and creative ideas are the foundation of the future. It is worth remembering that in Harry Alder's *Think Like a Leader*, a study of top British businessmen, he found that they identified right-brain thinking as the main reason for their success.

The DNA of our lives

Our visions can be centred around the kind of person we want to be rather than what we want to do. It can be a vision of the way we want to live our lives and the personal philosophies we want to adopt, rather than a vision describing imaginative goals. In his book *First Things First*, Stephen Covey describes the passion of vision:

'When we talk about "the passion of vision", we're talking about a deep, sustained energy that comes from a comprehensive, principle-based, need-based, endowment-based *seeing* … It taps into the deep core of who we are and what we are about. It is fuelled by the realisation of the unique contribution we have the capacity to make – the legacy we can leave. It clarifies purpose, gives direction, and empowers us to perform beyond our resources. We call it "passion" because this vision can become a motivating force so powerful it, in effect, becomes the DNA of our lives.'

I enjoyed my interview with Heather Rabbatts immensely because she has a very contagious passion for what she does. DNA is a very good way of describing her personal qualities.

'I think it's partly out of my sense of passion, I think it's the absolute belief that I can do things and make a difference. I won't get defeated by the system or whatever. I think I can make people laugh, I probably make them cry. I think there is a way you can conjure up emotions in other people. I'm bright and I think I can get to the heart of problems and solve them, I can say to people "what about this as a way forward?" and people who thought there was no way out, suddenly see there is light at the end of the tunnel.'

'In the end my passion was to make sure the business actually survived and what charisma I had left was actually persuading people to keep going.'

Paul Lever

Journey to the centre of the onion – *again?*

Vision and value systems; that is, having a vision of our future and what is valuable and important in our lives, are inextricably linked together.

Remember the onion? The outer layer represents the environment which we have created for ourselves or live within. The next two cover the way we behave and the skills we have developed. The fourth layer of the onion is the beliefs layer – the beliefs we absorbed from family and environment and those we have developed as a result of experience. Our beliefs are very important to us and we might talk about them occasionally, but for most of us this is not an everyday occurrence! Test this out. How much do you know about the beliefs of your family, friends and acquaintances? Do you *know* or do you just assume that they believe certain things? How many of us work on our beliefs? For example, do you believe the same things about your religion as you did when you were at school? We change our views on a wide variety of issues as we reach adulthood. As we develop critical faculties and as we acquire knowledge and understanding our world expands. But have we worked on our personal, religious and spiritual beliefs in the same way, or do we still have a 14-year-old's understanding of things religious and spiritual?

We very rarely, if ever, talk about our spirituality. Religion fits into the beliefs and behaviour layers of the onion. Spirituality is the core of our being – what makes us tick. If you are a humanist then you will believe that the energy we all have is generated within us and there is nothing else. If you believe in a greater being, who may be called God, One, the Universe or the Greater Self, then you may believe that this energy flows into us from outside or that we connect with this energy force and work to become absorbed into it. The Reverend Peter Timms is driven by his belief in God, which enables him to make his outstanding contribution to prisoner's welfare. Passion and enthusiasm surrounds him. Cynthia Homer is firmly convinced of the spiritual dimension to her work, as is Mo Acland. First, Cynthia Homer:

'You say that people felt I have charisma but I don't feel that there is anything special about myself. I hope I am a channel. For me, there is a very spiritual element which is the root of the whole thing.'

'There is something spiritual about charisma because it is the integrity of the whole. When you come up against flaws, disillusion steps in. It is very disappointing when people who appear to be charismatic professionally have sordid private lives.'

Mo Acland

'It is not a religious component but a spiritual component. It's about constantly being in touch with and updating what the meaning of your life is about.'

Dame Rennie Fritchie

Sprituality can be demonstrated by the way we behave towards other people. This was made very clear to me in the space of two days just as I was putting the finishing touches to this book. Joan Bookham, retired Vice Principal of my Alma Mater, Hereford College of Education, said that she felt people demonstrated their spirituality through their behaviour. Spirituality wasn't necessarily associated with religious activities. The next day I heard Anita Roddick talking to Bel Mooney on Radio 4 saying that for her serving humanity was a demonstration of spirituality.

On the whole, society's understanding of spiritually is very underdeveloped. And what of the business community?

'The spiritual side is regularly found to be missing in business management because the business world is still embryonic, in its pre-infancy. Because business is seen as "hard" and art and culture and spirituality are "soft", people think that you can't have both at the same time. You can. You should!'

Tony Buzan

WE ARE ALL EXPLORERS

We do know about loss of personal identity. This can happen if we have relied upon particular roles to describe our personal identity – mother, managing director, sales executive, policeman, teacher or steel worker. This reliance is quite understandable but can cause real problems if we are unaware that the roles we play mask the necessity for us to really find out who we are. This can happen if we are made redundant, when our children leave home, when we get left behind in the rat race or when we look back on our lives and realise that we may not have much time left. Excessive stress may cause us to think about our lives and the value of what we have been doing. This crisis of confidence may shake us to our very foundations. It may have happened to us or to people we know, but we are not particularly comfortable talking about it with our friends. We might be seen as neurotic, unstable and confused or, if you are a woman, menopausal or suffering from PMT! And yet our sense of identity is fundamental to our well-being and comfort. We have to learn that our sense of identity comes from who we are as a person. It does not lie in the roles that we play in life. If such a view were more acceptable, redundancy would be less painful, children leaving home would be less traumatic. Work and the role it provides enable us to reflect parts of ourselves, give us opportunities to contribute, and earn respect and dignity. But defining ourselves entirely through work and roles is dangerous. They are ephemeral and transitory parts of our lives. Both can be destroyed at one stroke. We only have to pick up a daily newspaper to see the truth of this.

We need to have confidence in who we are, to feel at peace with ourselves. It takes courage to explore ourselves and we should not underestimate the importance of support from friends and family as we embark on our journey to self-awareness. And, most importantly, we should not feel alone. It happens to many many people and it can be a wonderful but painful, fascinating and most difficult journey, all at the same time. Benedict Allen talked a lot about self-exploration.

> 'Everyone, even though they call me mad, would like to do what I do. We all are explorers. I don't mean that we all want to get on our rucksacks and go. I think that we all are pushing our own frontiers all the time. We're looking for ways of making our lives better and understanding the world. Some people have a religious faith and that maybe helps that portion of their world. Even if you believe for instance in a Christian type of God, it still doesn't answer all sorts of questions like infinity and space and so on, so there's always that element of discovery that's in all of us. I think that's why I appeal to a certain person. I also think the key to discovery is making yourself vulnerable. If you can have the courage to open yourself up then you will let that world in and that is when you start exploring. Exploration, to me, is all about learning and listening and not imposing.'

Wise words.

What is the difference between values and principles?

Principles are fundamental truths. They are general laws that govern the quality of our lives. They can be embodied in differing religious beliefs and represent the commonality between the different religions of the world. Principles are the natural systems which create the quality of our lives, like cause and effect: 'as ye sow, so shall ye reap'. For example, service and reciprocity; work and reward. Understanding the differences between principles and values is very important. Our *values*, which *repre-*

sent the things that are important to us, may be at odds with natural principles and we may need to reappraise our values to bring them into line. We might value money and material possessions more than family ties and friendship, for example. We need to think these things through and evaluate our values against natural principles. Ned Herrmann in his book *The Whole Brain Business Book* has devised a most helpful value clarification exercise, the essence of which is included below:

Value clarification exercise

1. What is most important in life for you? Write down ten or so items.
2. Rank your items in order of importance.
3. Review your list. Are you sure you have them in the right order? If not, change the order until you are satisfied.
4. Write down five or six reasons why you have put item 1 at the top of your list. Review this list after a few minutes.
5. Select the first supporting reason you have written down in step 4. Explore why you have put this down as the most important reason. Write down why you elected this as the most important reason.
6. Repeat steps 3–5 on the basis of the second most important item on your list. Go back and look at what you have written so far. Are there any common themes?

Using the work you have done so far, write a short statement describing your most important values.

Read your statement out loud to yourself several times. Are you expressing what is most important to you in your life? If so, these are your values.

I hear some of my readers muttering about all this soft stuff! Over the last few years I have had the privilege of working with many young managers, most of them men. I've found that behind the bluff boisterous 'young turk' image that many of them like to portray lies the much 'softer' side of their personalities waiting for permission to emerge. If I start the discussion around values and spirituality, for example, they will pick it up and run with it very happily. In my experience this kind of discussion rarely happens without a third party saying it's OK to discuss such things. Why is this so? I suspect that it's because their senior managers do not talk about these more private issues and consequently do not give them value in the world of work. There are plenty of senior managers who do think that these things are important, though. Peter Sharpe says that he's

'... always had values and I'm very keen to ensure people know my values. So again whether it's a young sergeant I'm promoting, I will tell him my expectations of him, I will also tell him what he can expect of me and that my behaviour will align to these values, to openness, to trust, to being reasonable. Passion, yes. Strategy, energy ... somewhere in there, there has to be something about being big enough to say, 'I'm sorry I got it wrong'. Perhaps that comes under courage. I think that a leader or a boss has to be someone who is upfront enough to say, "Yeah, I'm sorry I've got that wrong, I'll do it again". But in my experience the ability to say I got it wrong is so powerful that you can almost turn a group, certainly an individual, in a very short space of time, from being very negative to becoming very positive. It's very powerful.'

Baroness Pitkeathley's values are very clear:

'I've always had a vision about injustices in society. I can remember very clearly the first time I felt this – I would be four or five years old. It was during the war. My grandmother told me how they were a very poor family, she had been widowed in the First World War. She had two children, both very sick, probably in the early 1920s. My mother and her younger brother had whooping cough. My grandmother had no money and the children were very ill and she was very anxious. She called the doctor and he stood in the doorway and said "Have you my fee?" before he looked at the children. She replied that she hadn't and he turned and walked away. That is not right by any standards.'

Write your own obituary

How do I find out what my vision is if it is not obvious? How can I find out what I want to do? An easier question might be 'What do I want to have achieved in my life? What do I want to be remembered for?' Try answering these questions by writing your own obituary (Churchill did!). What would you want said about you after your death? If we know what we want to have achieved at the end of our lives then we have a good idea of what we ought to be doing in the here and now. How many people on their deathbed wish they had spent more time in the office? This does help us put things into perspective. If you find the idea of writing your obituary too upsetting, try writing down what you would like someone to say about you at your retirement party. This is not quite so final but serves the same purpose – focusing the mind upon what is really important.

As we have seen, visions lead into missions and mission statements. People can have mission statements. Stephen Covey is a great exponent of the value of personal mission statements:

'What we're talking about here is not simply writing a statement of belief. We're talking about accessing and creating an open connection with the deep energy that comes from a well-defined, thoroughly integrated sense of purpose and meaning in life. We're talking about creating a powerful vision based on principles that ensure its achievability. We're talking about the sense of excitement and adventure that grows out of connecting with your unique purpose and the profound satisfaction that comes in fulfilling it.'

Mission statements are not easy to write. Companies spend ages working them out and then often commission a PR firm to put the words together (which seems very odd to me). Personal mission statements are no different. They need to be drafted and redrafted and still they may not be right. But what might a personal mission statement look like?

The example below comes from one of the people identified as charismatic in the KOC survey. It sets out how this particular individual wants to behave. It is a 'doing' statement.

Personal mission statement – first draft

Values

The values of importance to me are:

- Honesty
- Fairness and justice
- Integrity
- Active compassion for people
- Concern for animals and the environment
- Reliability.

I *will* always stand up and be counted.

Personal objectives

- To formulate a clear set of expectations of myself and to achieve these, rather than hold others' expectations of me as more important
- To act in line with my principles and not be surprised and hurt when others react adversely
- To live my life without damaging other people knowingly or intentionally in my personal or professional relationships
- To be there for my partner, my family and my friends, particularly in their difficult times

---

- To put fun, enjoyment and the unexpected into all my relationships.
- To make people I come into contact with feel 'special' and to reflect their worth to them through the way I relate to them
- To work at understanding myself.

Professional objectives

- To value the talents I have been given and to seek opportunities to use them for the benefit of others and the achievement of my own goals. I believe these talents are:
  — to communicate a passion for whatever I am engaged in
  — the ability to generate enthusiasm
  — creativity
  — good communication skills
  — an ability to deal with complexity of ideas and situations
  — leadership
  — energy.
- To enjoy, develop and maintain my enthusiasm for new ideas, learning and interest in a wide variety of areas
- To understand, acknowledge and continuously develop my 'scarce resource'
- To look forward positively and enthusiastically, enjoy the good things from the past, leaving the negative behind.

Overall

To live my life wholeheartedly, whatever I do.

How would your mission statement differ?

IT'S ALL ABOUT KNOWING YOUR ONIONS

Exploring and understanding ourselves helps to understand the concept of vision and all charismatic people have a vision. It is not always a grand vision; it might be on a smaller scale but everyone interviewed for this book has a personal vision. These visions are a guiding light in each life. There is no doubt that a sense of purpose, a vision of what we want to achieve in our lives, is important if we don't want to drift through life, hoping that things will work out right for us. Our sense of purpose can change over our lifetime and the challenge is to regain a sense of vision and purpose when doors close or we reach a specific goal. Sense of purpose does not just 'come' for most of us. We have to work very hard at it. More often than not, this means battling away with ourselves, trying to get to know ourselves better – trying to get to the centre of the onion. And if we don't try? We drift.

It's *never* too late

I often hear people saying, 'It's too late for me. I could never do that now'. Immediately I say, 'Well why don't you do it now. What's to stop you?' Recently I heard myself saying that I would have liked to have sung opera or oratorio. Hoisted with my own petard! I am now taking singing lessons. It's never too late to achieve your vision. Tony Buzan was quite clear about that:

> 'Torville and Dean had a vision. They saw star skaters on TV – they thought "That's it. That is what we want to do". The strength of the vision is very important as is the time you devote to realising it. For them it took extraordinary energy and tremendous dedication, but look what they achieved. Vision can develop at any time at all. Suddenly, at the age of 50 Gaugin said – "I want to paint". He'd seen paintings and wanted to do the same. Baden Powell had the idea for the Boy Scouts in his mid-50s. Vision can come at any time in life.'

One of the most difficult things to do is to separate out our own visions or wishes from other people's visions for us. As we grow up other people have expectations of us. They tell us about the things they want us to do, the places they want us to go and the kind of people they want us to be. Some people are very strong and can resist this conditioning very effectively – often because they do have a strong sense of purpose. Many of the rest of us conform to these expectations and can find ourselves in jobs we don't want to do and in relationships that do not suit us: square pegs in round holes. Eventually we must find our way out and find out what we really want in life. We need our own dreams and visions. They may be very simple ones and that is fine. Round pegs in round holes!

Many of the people I interviewed have had difficult and sometimes traumatic lives one way or another. With one exception, the one thing they all had in common was a strong sense of purpose, even though this purpose had changed and developed for many of them as their lives have progressed. One person I interviewed appeared to have lost their original purpose had not found another. This person was busy living in the past and on past glories. I felt a sense of drift and sadness. Our sense of purpose should not be entirely bound up with our professional work because most people's work comes to an end at sometime or other through retirement or redundancy. Our sense of purpose must transcend work and be rooted in ourselves. It really does all come back to the centre of the onion!

SUMMARY

- Charismatic individuals normally have a sense of personal vision and mission
- *Vision* — seeing things which do not currently exist
  - having imaginative insight
  - people have visions
- *Mission* — something to be done
  - people and organisations have missions
- Visions and missions can change and develop
- The passion of vision is the DNA of our lives
- Vision and values are inextricably linked together
- We rarely talk about our values and almost never talk about our spirituality
- We are all explorers of ourselves
- Writing a personal mission statement is a good way to define what you really stand for and what you really want in life.

Action points

- Set out on the journey of self-awareness
- Identify personal values and beliefs
- Assess these against natural principles
- Write your own obituary to give you guidance on what you want to achieve in your life
- Draw up a personal mission statement.

RATE YOURSELF ON CHARISMATIC COMMUNICATION SKILLS

1. On a scale of 1–4, rate the following managerial skills in order of importance
    - (a)   decision-making ☐
    - (b)   communication ☐
    - (c)   delegation ☐
    - (d)   project management ☐

2. At the end of the day, I believe that rational logical thought is the only acceptable way to think at work.
    - (a)   I agree ☐
    - (b)   I don't agree ☐

3. People usually think that my formal presentations are
    - (a)   excellent ☐
    - (b)   good ☐
    - (c)   average ☐
    - (d)   poor ☐

4. When I speak I always sound interesting
    - (a)   I don't think that I ever sound interesting ☐
    - (b)   most of the time ☐
    - (c)   yes, I do ☐
    - (d)   if what I am talking about is important it doesn't matter if I sound interesting or not ☐

5.   I know that I can inspire people when I want to
    - (a)   yes, I can ☐
    - (b)   sometimes ☐
    - (c)   I have no idea how to inspire anyone ☐

6. I take a great deal of care with my image
    - (a)   I don't think of my image at all ☐
    - (b)   yes, I am always dressed properly for every occasion ☐
    - (c)   I don't consciously think about my image but I am confident I look as I want to all the time ☐

7. I know that I have personal presence
    - (a)   no idea what is meant by this ☐
    - (b)   sometimes ☐
    - (c)   most of the time ☐
    - (d)   I know that I do not have personal presence ☐

8. I feel embarrassed when I hear people talking passionately and enthusiastically at work
   (a) depends on what they are talking about ☐
   (b) always ☐
   (c) never ☐

9. Instinct is not reliable
   (a) I agree. It is never reliable ☐
   (b) I disagree. It can be very reliable ☐

10. Humour is always appropriate
    (a) I agree. Humour always improves a situation ☐
    (b) I disagree. Humour can be counter-productive ☐

11. How many senses contribute to our ability to communicate?
    (a) two ☐
    (b) four ☐
    (c) five ☐
    (d) six ☐

Score

1. (a) 2nd 4	2. (a) 0	3. (a) 5	4. (a) 0	5. (a) 5	6. (a) 0
(b) 1st 10	(b) 5	(b) 4	(b) 4	(b) 4	(b) 3
(c) 3rd 2		(c) 3	(c) 5	(c) 0	(c) 5
(d) 3rd 2		(d) 1	(d) –1		

7. (a) 0	8. (a) 3	9. (a) 0	10. (a) 0	11. (a) –1
(b) 3	(b) –1	(b) 5	(b) 5	(b) 3
(c) 4	(c) 5			(c) 4
(d) 1				(d) 5

Score ☐

Total available: 60 marks. If you scored:

- Over 55   You have excellent communication skills.
- Between 40 and 55   You use your communication skills very well.
- Between 30 and 40   You need to improve your communication skills.
- Under 30   Much of your impact is lost. You need to understand the elements of good communication and then practise implementing your knowledge in your everyday interaction with people.

Key 3 THE COMMUNICATION KEY

Charismatics have one very valuable gift that most of us would do any-thing to acquire, so to speak. Fortunately, we all have it in various amounts and in various qualities. However, because it is as natural to us as breathing, it is easy to forget that it is a tender plant that needs lots of care if it is to grow. Charismatics recognise that they have it and work hard at making the most of it. They hone and refine it to incredible levels of effectiveness to suit their purposes. For most of us, it is the most valuable of our personal skills. No prizes for guessing that this most precious of gifts is the ability to communicate – the *Communication Key*.

My conversations with charismatic individuals highlighted the impor-tance of this skill for them. Communication is a huge topic and in describ-ing this third Key to Charisma I have concentrated on the aspects of communication which differentiate charismatic folk from the rest of us. Charismatic individuals have that something extra.

A manager who cannot communicate cannot manage anything. A leader who cannot communicate has no chance of leading anyone any-where. Different levels of communication skill differentiate the poor from the mediocre and the mediocre from the brilliant, be they manager or leader. It is important that all of us involved in leadership and manage-ment understand the communication process thoroughly. We need an appreciation of our own expertise in this area. Managing and leading means *engaging* with those we manage and lead. Individuals are identified as charismatic *because they engage in an exciting and magical way with others*. This third Key – Communication – analyses the special way in which charismatics engage with others. What is it that they do in addition to being pretty good at the more familiar skills of communication – listening, knowing when to be assertive, and managing conflict, for example?

WHAT DOES COMMUNICATION MEAN?

To communicate means to 'impart information *and evoke understanding*': that is, to inspire feelings, energies and, above all, a response from others. That is done with energy, passion and enthusiasm; all these qualities are expressed through body language and tone of voice, not words. Commu-nication is not just what we say – it is how we say it. It is a two-way process. Evelyn Glennie has special memories of a particularly brilliant communicator:

'I think one of the great communicators that I've learnt from over the years is James Blades – the grandfather of percussion. He can perform without instruments. Whether he is speaking to a five-year-old or a 95-year-old he injects real excitement. That is so special. I remember meeting him the first time when I was 14 years old, and at that time he would have been in his late 70s/early 80s. I walked into the hall and saw this old man and thought "Oh boy" … but we were all just transfixed. He was really magic.'

'If you can't communicate you can't express what charisma you might have.'

Paul Lever

Peter Sharpe described the way that Sir John Harvey Jones engages with people:

'I suppose John Harvey Jones is everybody's ideal. For me he gets on people's wavelength, he gets people talking, he gets underneath them and understands them and listens to what they have to say. His intellectual ability and the experiences that he's had enable him to take the information he has been given and link it to the business. He can give a consultant's view immediately. He is a very charismatic character.'

'I think charismatic people really have the commitment to communicate properly and they are generous about it. They want to give and to receive all the time.'

Nancy Wise

Benedict Allen put it another way:

'A lot of these people that I find personally charismatic have another element to them and that is an ability to communicate. They have something to say, and they have the ability to say it. I think some people use very few words to do it but they have a sort of quietness about them. Other people have a noisiness about them. The noisy people tend to express themselves directly and your attention is drawn to them because they're zapping you with their energy.

The quiet people have a quiet dignity, and you're drawn to them. It's almost as if they have this force field around them and your attention is drawn to them, not just because they are sending out this sort of energy but because they have also created a space around themselves.'

WHAT IS SPECIAL ABOUT CHARISMATIC COMMUNICATION?

The real meaning of communication is the response that is achieved. Communication skills are used to influence people and charismatic individuals are very good at this. Unfortunately, influencing people can be seen as manipulation, and this has negative connotations (back to Hitler?) – manipulation smacks of getting people to do things that they do not want to! Recalling his days at Eton, Sir Antony Acland remembers the former Dean of Durham coming down during the Easter term to preach in chapel in Holy Week. He was the best preacher Sir Antony had ever heard. The Dean would get out of his stall and limp very slowly up the aisle. He was a tremendously handsome man. All the lights would go out, two by two, leaving just the candles on the pulpit and the candles on the altar – everywhere else was in total darkness. The Dean's voice came over just loud enough to be heard if nobody fidgeted ... and he held the place spellbound for 20 minutes: boys, masters and visitors, all alike. Sir Antony recalls going out into the cold night and wondering if they hadn't all been cheated by a performance. Everyone was tremendously impressed but was it all contrived? Was the Dean's performance planned? In later years Sir Antony asked the Dean's daughter, Elizabeth Home, if her father planned his sermons to be like this. Was it all an act? She said she thought no. She knew he had this power, this magnetism. He had a natural talent. He didn't sit down and plan the lights going out and the limp and so on – it just happened naturally.

An ability to communicate and span the years in such a way as this is truly effective communication. After 35 years I can remember many of my teachers' lessons very clearly. I count myself fortunate that I was part of a generation which had the benefit of the very many charismatic individuals who entered the teaching profession after the war and before the multiplicity of careers beckoned.

For me, the message is to be less sceptical.

If you didn't already know this ...

The real meaning of our words is expressed through the tone of our voice, our body language and paralanguage – the combination of signals we give out when we speak, apart from the words themselves.

Amazingly enough,

- 55 per cent of the impact of a presentation is made by our body language posture, gestures and eye contact,
- 38 per cent by the tone of our voices and
- only 7 per cent by the actual content of the presentation.

There will be differences depending on the type of presentation but the message is clear – words are normally less important than body language and tone of voice. When preparing formal presentations we tend to spend the bulk of the time preparing the words and very little working out how we should deliver them. We might achieve greater success if we reversed things and spent more time on the delivery and less on the words!

It is very easy to become complacent and think that our skills and expertise are adequate and there is no need for improvement. This tends to be a very common view among those at the top of the managerial hierarchy. Many feel that they have 'done it all before' and 'not got time' to waste on further training and development, and certainly not on *interpersonal skills*! We often hear, 'If I wasn't a good communicator, I wouldn't be in my present post.' Poppycock! Employees on communication skills programmes always express the same complaint – the course should be run for their senior managers rather than for them. (On the quiet I normally agree with them.) Communication skills courses usually cover aspects such as interpersonal skills, listening skills, giving and receiving feedback, the importance of body language, formal presentation skills and assertiveness. Perhaps people are rather insulted by the implication that they need to develop these very basic but vital skills. Personally, I want to be as good as I can be at all of these – which means continuous learning and practice. My charismatic interviewees all said that they never stopped learning.

A soft option?

Many men think interpersonal skills courses are a joke, a soft option, and not to be taken too seriously. They prefer to associate themselves with the 'hard' business areas, such as accounting and project management. Women, on the other hand, will normally opt for interpersonal skills courses rather than tackling the harder issues. This becomes obvious at conferences where delegates have a choice of workshop sessions; workshops will be over- or under-subscribed depending on the dominant sex at the conference. This might be because delegates feel confident in particular areas or convince themselves that a particular workshop will be more beneficial. The truth is more likely to lie in the underlying attitudes to the topics themselves. Most men dramatically undervalue the vital importance of developing effective interpersonal skills and women still struggle against ingrained ideas that the hard areas of business are for men only.

How did *you* rate on the communication questionnaire?

I want to concentrate on the aspects of communication that make people memorable and charismatic. What are these? The first of these has to be the ability to communicate with passion and feeling.

Passion and feeling through language and voice

We all possess a most sophisticated musical instrument – our voice. The importance of this is easily forgotten. Sir Ian McKellen, Dame Judi Dench and Eartha Kitt, all identified as charismatic, are masters of their voices, as were Sir Winston Churchill and Martin Luther King. Barry John suggested that his Welsh voice almost demanded that people notice him:

'Amazingly I've found if I go to places like England, half the time it's my accent that attracts people, not what I say.'

Most charismatic individuals leave an indelible impression on their audiences and, as we might expect, it is not normally the words alone that create the impression, but their tone of voice, their passion and the way they deliver the message. They convey excitement and magic through their voices. Patsy Rosenburg, Head of the Voice Department at the Royal National Theatre, hints that if we do not use our voices to express what we want to say with feeling, whatever those feelings may be, we are in danger of projecting ourselves as empty, unfulfilled and quite superficial:

'The voice is totally dependent on a speaker's moods, energy and intellect. The voice is actually a fine barometer of the atmospheric pressure within someone's body or life. Effective communication is not just about a well-pronounced sound ... If we never allow our feelings, thoughts or imagination to enter our voices, the whole vocal production process will sound empty, unfulfilled and quite superficial. To get slightly mystical for a moment, the voice is an instrument that echoes the soul and it is the soul's energy that makes every sound unique ... Love, grief, rage, joy, laughter, foolishness or just simple curiosity can stir this inner energy and stimulate the voice into action. Vocal imagination, I think, getting in touch with the soul of whatever you are trying to say, is the first place to start working with the voice.'

Grethe Hooper Hanson wrote me recently:

'It's a pity you couldn't make the SEAL Conference, which featured some pretty powerful charismatics, all of whom I regarded with different eyes since talking to you! Barbara Meister Vitale had her audiences virtually hypnotised most of the time, though perhaps the most powerful of them all was Veronica Andres from Argentina, who embodies Latin passion and definitely has the Evita touch. However, I was at a seminar with Lozanov in Sweden in February at which he warned us all against the temptation of charismatics, which, he maintained, lower the autonomy of the receiver. An interesting thought.'

Charismatic individuals communicate passionately, albeit sometimes quietly, but always enthusiastically.

Stiff upper lip is 'out', showing you care is 'in'

Good managers used to be seen as rational and unemotional, objective and logical and organisations normally reward people for behaving in this way. Fortunately, we are moving towards a more balanced view where passion, feelings and creativity are just as important. But it's hard to shake off the old habits of not showing our feelings. It is worth asking yourself the question, 'How do I as a manager show that I care?' Sir John Harvey Jones put it this way:

> 'When I talk to large groups of people, which I do a lot, I am very conscious that the first job that I have to do is to build a common bridge of empathy with them. I usually do this by making a joke at my own expense or whatever it may be. Once you have built an emotional bridge, and it has to be an emotional bridge, then you open up the lines of communication. Communication is much more about emotion than it is about fact. If there is anything in this at all, it is the fact that one is prepared to show one's emotions and that of course, for an English man or woman is a highly risky job, as we know. I don't think you can communicate with anybody unless you communicate on an emotional level, and that means that you have to take the risk that they will, metaphorically, kick you in the back, think you are a wimp, think you are stupid or that you are making a pass or any one of a thousand undesirable things. That's the risk you have to take in order to communicate at all.'

Industry? That's borrrring ...

Be honest and ask yourself how often you describe your work with energy and passion. How often do any of us really give the impression of enthusiasm through what we say and how we say it? Do we give the impression that we *like* what we do? Sadly its 'not done' to be enthusiastic. Most group norms require us to be non-committal and rather uninterested in our work. It is no wonder that the children, described in the introduction to this book, when asked about their views on work said that work was boring. Fortunately, there are people and organisations who behave in quite the opposite way. One of the things that struck me most forcibly when I visited a number of my charismatic interviewees was the aura of energy and enthusiasm that surrounded not only the person themselves, but their organisations. I remember stepping into Reverend Peter

Timms' organisation and hitting a wave of enthusiasm. It was just like going from London to Dar es Salaam, getting out of the plane and being engulfed by the tropical African heat.

Of course, there are examples of passion and enthusiasm in industry and commerce. Richard Branson is very passionate about the products and services he provides, as is Anita Roddick of Body Shop. Successful salespeople are successful because they are passionate about their products and services, not because of the quality of what they are selling. We know this because people will buy rubbish from charlatans and 'wide boys' because they are passionate and enthusiastic. Of course, many of the charlatans and wide boys are charismatic too!

Sir Antony Acland thinks that understating emotion is part of the British way of life. He thinks that this is a great mistake. There is no advantage in being over-emotional, but men should be able to weep as well as women. It is probably something people can learn, and it is to do with taking an interest in others, being sensitive and not being too self-centred. He says that sometimes you can see what leadership is about by examining the common failures of leadership: complacency, lack of vision, lack of feeling and lack of care.

'There are two big charismatic musical influences for me. One was the late Jacqueline du Pré – she was extraordinary as a musician. You mention the passion and the bubbliness. For me she was definitely extraordinary. I never forget reading somewhere that someone said that she plays in too much of an exaggerated and passionate form. Barbirolli the conductor replied, saying "Oh my God! She's a nineteen year old, she's a teenager! Let her be a teenager, that's what teenagers are about, they're young and vivacious!" I thought yes, you have to play as honestly as you possibly can whatever age you are.'

Evelyn Glennie

People often say to me, 'But I *am* keen. I am enthusiastic about it. Why don't people believe me when I talk about it?' Probably because they sound ... dead boring! (I don't say that to them, of course.) Imagine that your voice is connected up to a monitor similar to the heart monitors that we see so often in medical dramas, where life is represented by a moving line on the monitor. Suddenly, there is a 'ping'. The line moves straight across the monitor without any inflection, turns into a white dot and ... disappears. The patient has expired – dead. Dead boring! Putting tone, speed and colour into our voices is vital if we want people to listen. An endless monotone is enough to turn even the keenest listener right off. It is just too difficult to listen to. But charismatic speech has more than just tone, speed and colour. It involves speed of delivery.

John Heron, an eminent psychologist, describes the way we speak in two kinds of speaking time – clock time and charismatic time. Clock time speed is the one we use most of the time when we are communicating formally. It is made up of dense amounts of words delivered in a way which convey information, opinion and belief. We talk non-stop in fairly long bursts. This looks like a jagged line crossing the monitor.

Charismatic time, on the other hand, would flow across the monitor in waves:

Charismatic speech is deep rhythm speech. It means using our voices as a projection of our living presence. It contains pauses and silences. Both are used to create rhythm and emphasis, intention and awareness. The tone of voice is much richer, and the language more poetic. We are really *engaged* with our listeners rather than just delivering words. Two good examples of speakers using charismatic time would be Churchill's 'We shall fight them on the beaches' speech and Martin Luther King's 'I have a dream' speech.

CHARISMATIC FOLK ARE *ELECTRIC*

It is worth exploring what Heron means by 'living presence'. He distinguishes between two kinds of body: our experiential bodies and our physical bodies. The physical body describes what we look like from the outside – what we can see of ourselves in the mirror, what we glean from other people's feedback on our physical appearance. Experiential bodies are quite different. This is our inner body image, the one we live in, the one we 'feel'. It is being conscious of ourselves and the space we occupy. We become aware of every bit of ourselves from our toes to the top of our heads and beyond. Some people would call the latter our 'aura'. This gives us personal presence. Some people have never had this feeling and certainly can't feel it at will. But some people have the ability to walk into a room and make it fall silent. This is very powerful personal presence; and personal presence is the foundation of charisma. This concept was well illustrated by one of my interviewees:

> 'Making presentations gives me a real buzz. When I stand up to speak I can feel myself relaxing. I can feel the energy all over my body. I stand up straight. I look all around the room. I am not in any hurry. It all goes quiet and I know that I have everyone's attention.

> If I don't have this I consciously project my presence into the audience. I wait and the room goes quiet until everyone is looking at me with expectation. If it is a very large audience I can feel myself turning up the "power", turning the dimmer switch to full light, projecting my energy all about me. I am not frightened at all. I know that I can do it. And the belief and power comes from inside me. I feel in complete control.

> For me, it's not what I say that matters to me. It is passion, energy and enthusiasm that I want to leave behind. That is what I want the audience to remember. They will work out the specific content for themselves.'

Tony Buzan commented on posture as well:

> 'Charisma is also reflected in posture. When charismatics begin to talk about what it is that impassions them, you will notice that their posture changes. They become more upright, more poised and in all ways both physically and mentally more open and expansive.'

In the first quote my interviewee is also talking about the ability to inspire – another of the gifts that all charismatics have.

Inspiration: infuse thought or feeling into, to animate, to breathe in.

> Did you ever know that you are my hero?
> And everything I wish I could be
> I can fly higher than an eagle
> You are the wind beneath my wings.
> *Written by Larry Henley and Jeff Silbar, sung*
> *by Bette Midler*

Human beings have always been a source of inspiration for each other, some more than others, and none more so than the charismatic individuals who have inspired their followers down the centuries. Now, in the late twentieth century, Bette Midler likens the source of her inspiration to the 'wind' – not so very far from early Christian writings describing the Holy Ghost as a 'rushing mighty wind'. Both reflect the meaning of the word 'inspiration' – drawing in breath. To inspire means to animate and infuse with thought and feelings and that, of course, is just what it feels like when we are influenced by charismatic individuals. They are able to do just that, filling us with enthusiasm (a word which itself means 'possessed by God') and passion for their particular point of view or cause. They can make us feel really good and uplifted. They can almost *give* us their energy. The ability to do this demonstrates communication skills at their very best. Pia Helena Ormerod put it like this:

> 'Charisma is a word that should only be used for people who, through their strong personality, can inspire people to find something within themselves they didn't think they had. It may be through work, or through a religious experience, shared dreams or aspirations, but they find something within themselves that they didn't think they had.'

Edwina Currie adds:

> 'A charismatic person inspires confidence that he or she will see it through, whatever the odds. That force of character, determination and will-power alone will carry us all through. Those who are listening are invited to join the crusade.'

We all have the ability to inspire others in different ways. Charismatic individuals understand this and consciously develop their skills in this area. However, as with all other potentially dangerous skills we need to use them with great care. Of course, things can go wrong – but they can go right, too! Potential danger is not a reason for suppressing or leaving our talents undeveloped in this area.

What are the real secrets of inspiration? Quite simply, passion and enthusiasm, however they are manifested. Courage and example. Sharing a vision. Very often the passion and enthusiasm may be for what lies within another person and not what we see on the outside. Evelyn Glennie and Edwina Currie had a lot to say about inspiration:

> 'I think people do find inspiration in what I do and whether I like that or not it happens. What I do to make them feel that I don't know. I think it's just a combination of things. I think different aspects of what I do appeals to different people. Sometimes it is because I am a woman although I don't like getting into that sort of issue. Or it can be quite simply that they want to do the same kind of thing as I do. Of course the deafness aspect is a tremendous inspiration to a lot of young people who want to be musicians, or anything else for that matter and that's quite important. And then there is the kind of inspiration that you can't quite put into words where people go along to your concerts and they just feel excited by it but they don't know why. It's just a combination of things. For example, drumming has this macho image but suddenly people feel inspired seeing a women there making music out of drums. It's hard to say what it really is.'
>
> *Evelyn Glennie*

'A charismatic person also inspires confidence, a confidence beyond evidence, that he or she can do this, that whatever the odds they would see it through. That force of character and determination and will-power alone will carry us all through and that therefore those who are listening are invited to join the crusade. The very fact that lots of people enjoy the crusade makes success more likely. A charismatic person often carries with them the seed of success where a more ordinary person wouldn't, even though their ideas may be much the same.'

Edwina Currie

'I quite regularly have people asking for a one-to-one conversation and I do quite a lot of executive coaching. Afterwards people come back and say "you inspired me to …" So the word "inspired" comes up a lot – for me that's part of charisma. I don't consciously inspire. I do it because it's my only way of communicating my total belief in the other person's ability to continue to develop.'

Dame Rennie Fritchie

Many of us, particularly if we are over 40, remember teachers who inspired us. I wondered if today's students enjoy the same opportunities. I asked Christine Dipple, headmistress of Talbot Heath School, what she thought. She replied:

'I think we have more efficient teachers, but I don't think there is room any more for the inspirational oddities. Not in the same way there was; usually those people were inefficient in some ways, perhaps because they weren't very good at getting their reports in on time or they weren't very good at doing the paperwork. There may be some room for independence but I can't see there's any room in the state system for this. I think there are subjects which provide platforms for inspiration – English for instance, French literature. The teacher I remember best was a master who went round shouting; he was really an awful teacher but he inspired in all of us a love of enlightenment. But I don't think he was a good teacher.'

I found this very sad, and I hope that she is wrong.

Sir Antony Acland remembers Lady Thatcher's ability to inspire. If she said 'Charge', people would hear her voice, and she'd inspire them and they would go.

But isn't all this passion and feeling just acting?

In case we should think that acting is all sham and make-believe, Sir Peter Hall, former Director of the National Theatre and founder of the Peter Hall Company, describes the issues that face actors when they are using the masks required in ancient Greek theatre:

> 'By the use of a mask, the actor can change his age, his bearing, his physique – even his sexuality. He can express areas of his personality he did not know existed. But they are nonetheless parts of him, otherwise he is pretending and being false. True acting is a revelation of the self, not an imitation of somebody else.'

Managers must be actors, but no one is asking us to pretend. It's about showing our own feelings.

So far, I have concentrated on sending information – but what is special about a charismatic individual's ability to receive information?

Special sensitive antennae

One of the best ways of describing the way we receive information is through the analogy of wide band and narrow band receiving: see Figure 1. Listening to the words and concentrating on the narrow band only ensures that we receive the obvious content of what is being communicated but miss the more accurate fine detail of the message. Learning to tune in to the complete transmission ensures that we receive all the information available – then nothing should come as a surprise. How often do we hear the comment, 'Well, I'm not a mind reader, am I?' But many people seem to be. We all have the capacity to gather far more information from people than we currently do, and the easiest way to start to tune in more effectively is to develop our sense of caring for other people. Without exception, all the charismatic people I interviewed stressed the importance of thinking about other people, anticipating their needs and working to help others achieve their goals. Heather Rabbatts, the CEO of Lambeth Borough Council, emphasised the importance of talking to people, listening to what they say and anticipating their needs.

Paul Lever, Sir John Harvey Jones, Sir John Acland, Evelyn Glennie, Dame Rennie Fritchie, Barry John – in fact, *all* the people I interviewed – said that listening to people and showing them that you cared was the one most important thing that they tried to do all the time. It was one of the secrets of their success. In particular, Sir Antony Acland felt that a good leader must be a good listener, and he used the phrase, 'sensitive antennae which enable them to pick up anxieties'.

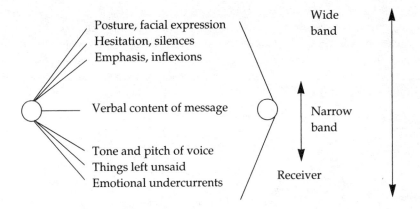

Figure 1: *Listening on the wide band*

Source: P and J Hodgson, Effective Meetings

A sixth sense?

John Heron thinks that we all have another method of receiving information – intrasensory perception, or ISP. He describes this as 'the non-sensory perception of the other's mental and emotional state, which is interwoven with sensory apprehension but cannot be reduced to it'. He means the ability to receive more information than can actually be perceived through our normal senses: in other words, a person's ability to connect with another's energy field – the 'sixth sense'. This isn't the same as *extra*sensory perception, or ESP. ESP, if you believe in its existence, includes such things as telepathy and clairvoyance. *Intra* – meaning between – sensory perception means that extra information passes between two people or groups who are physically close to one another. Two of my interviewees gave good examples of ISP:

> 'I believe I often know how she is feeling. I'm sure I do. I cannot see her and she cannot see me even though I am near her. I can almost sense her facial expressions sometimes. I feel when she is really interested and feels well. I suspect that I know when she has a headache. How do I know? I can't tell you, but I know that I know. It may be that I have the time and opportunity to be still and be open to another person when I am in this situation.'

> 'I know what he is thinking. We often come out with exactly the same thought at the same time. It can be rather unnerving but it is also very reassuring. I always know if something is wrong without him having to say anything.'

We all have this sixth sense, but not all of us are tuned in to it. We don't give ourselves the chance to use it. This is normally because we are more concerned with ourselves than with the other person. Skaters Jane Torville and Christopher Dean must be real masters of ISP. Nothing else can account for their incredible performances. They are perfectly in tune with one another on the ice.

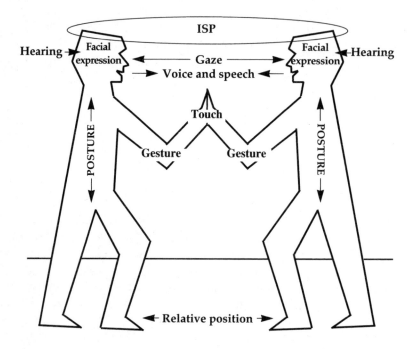

Figure 2: *Diagram illustrating ISP, together with other more commonly understood ways of relating to others*

Source: John Heron, Group Facilitation

I have described ISP because it appears to offer an explanation of how many charismatic individuals are able to sense the needs of others so easily. They can open themselves up to others and focus on other people in depth rather than on themselves. This means that those who use the gift wisely can respond to other people's unspoken needs as if by magic. However, if you feel that the concept of ISP is just too far-fetched, what about intuition or gut feeling? However, not everyone thinks that this is to be trusted as a source of information, because it isn't logical or rational. Women have always used this particular sense even though it has not always been appreciated by male colleagues! In Harry Alder's survey of successful CEOs many of them rated intuition very highly. Many attributed their success to their willingness to act on intuition.

I asked Sir Antony Acland to tell me more about his intuition and how it works for him. He thinks his intuition is based on his ability to listen. He stressed the importance of being interested, of keeping his ears open, and being out and about. He 'wanders around' and talks to his staff, putting them at their ease. He is then able to pick up nuance and information. He thinks it is difficult at the top of the pyramid, whether you are Home Secretary, Permanent Under-Secretary of the Foreign Office, Ambassador to Washington or the Provost of Eton, because people are often reluctant to tell you things, thinking of you as a sort of great panjandrum they dare not risk upsetting. But he thinks you can overcome this in any environment by showing a friendly interest and just being sensitive to the warning signs.

Charismatic individuals often look different

Michael Heseltine's flowing locks, Sir John Harvey Jones' flamboyant ties, Dr Gordon Wills' necklace, Edwina Currie's brilliant colours, Evelyn Glennie's skin-tight outfits, Nigel Kennedy's earring and headscarf and Richard Branson's woolly pullovers suggest that anything goes. It does, if you have a thick enough skin to brazen it out and the confidence to pull it off – and you have what people want. Dr Gordon Wills, Principal of the International Management Centres, has worn a silver necklace outside his shirt and under his tie for many years. He started to do this in the early 1980s when jewellery for men was still thought rather cissy and unacceptable in business situations. He put up with comments from his students at Cranfield where he was Professor of Marketing at the time; later his colleagues at IMC frequently fielded questions on the subject from clients. Gordon's dress sense has often caused comment. It is not just anyone who can attend a formal black tie occasion in America in a bush jacket and casual trousers. Nothing appears to put him off. He does his own thing and his idiosyncratic image has done little to hinder his success as a businessman, although his academic peers have found both him and his image much more difficult to cope with. Gore Vidal said, 'Style is knowing who you are, what you want to say and not giving a damn!' That describes Gordon Wills to a T.

Listen to the Queen's Press Secretary

In his book *Personal Impact: The Art of Good Communication*, Michael Shea comes down firmly on the side of clothes being a powerful way of communicating without speaking. He says that it is not just what, but how you wear what you wear that counts. As the Queen's Press Secretary at home with the influential for many years, he should know. He gives some useful hints:

- Feeling and looking smart gives confidence
- Dress more formally if you want to project an image of control and serious authority
- Develop a sophisticated bearing by looking at how peers and senior people present themselves
- Dress with propriety and follow the unwritten rules – or be prepared to take the consequences
- Pay attention to details like clean nails and shoes, and pressed clothes.

Obvious, yes – but perhaps a little boring! And boring is just what charismatic people are not. Charismatic people develop a sense of their own personal identity which is more important to them than wearing the accepted uniform of the day. They do not normally outrage their audiences – but neither will they conform to other people's views of how they should look. Benedict Allen had a number of problems with organisers of dinners and conferences, who wanted him to wear the accepted uniform of a formal suit on these occasions. He has steadfastly refused to conform and has developed a dress sense that makes him feel comfortable. In a letter Benedict wrote to me after making a presentation to a large school he said:

> 'At the school I wore a formal suit – I think the only thing to do for a prize-giving occasion. I felt fine: it's a slightly tropical suit and unusual (which sums me up fairly well, as well!).'

What you have to offer has to outweigh the prejudices of your audiences. Everyone has prejudices. It *is* important to understand what you can and cannot do. Of course, you incur risks by not conforming, but there are greater risks in cramping one's style and personality into an image which does not fit. Who wants to be a grey man in a grey suit? The Chief Constable of Hertfordshire, Peter Sharpe, does not wear grey suits. His wife will not let him because of the image that they conjure up, even though his personality is such that no one could ever describe him as 'grey'.

Read the books, observe colleagues and ensure you know how image is created and what is expected in all situations. Then decide what image *you* want to project and work out how to do it. If you want to buck the system make sure you have the courage, stature and standing to do it. If, on reflection, you feel that you haven't, tone your ideas down but don't give them up. Wait for the right opportunity, then go for it. Sir Antony Acland who, as a former Head of the Foreign Office and now Provost of Eton, is a doyen of the Establishment, believes that we need *more* flamboyance, not less – which is very encouraging.

The lighter side of life

Most charismatics are very good-humoured most of the time, and have a well-developed sense of humour. My initial list of charismatic qualities did not include humour, but time and time again my interviewees said that this should be added because it was very important. They felt that it is important not to take life too seriously, and to be able to laugh at oneself. Many of them said that they tried hard to be fun to be with. They liked cracking jokes and laughing with those around them. True, we can't all be the life and soul of the party, but we can all appreciate other people's good humour and encourage all around us to see work as fun. Life is a serious business, but we do not have to make it any more serious than it already is. Treating matters in a light-hearted fashion does not mean that we are belittling their importance. What it does mean is that that we have a better chance of getting things into perspective. Humour, it must not be misplaced, nor used at anyone else's expense. It must also be used in context and with due regard to the environment and the recipients.

Would you describe yourself as fun to be with? Do you have fun at work? Is your life fun?

Most of us are weighed down with the cares and sorrows of the world, described by the media every morning without fail. Tony Buzan was very critical of the media and its influence on the nation's thinking:

> 'If every journalist knew how the brain works and how delicate and powerful it is they would change their approach when presenting information to the world. They would realise that if you keep filling the brain with negative information everyday you are not surprisingly going to depress it and fill it with misinformation. It's like having a beautiful lake in which you are continually dumping pollution. Eventually that lake finds it very hard to support a life system. For example, I used to wake up in the morning to the news and I would wonder why everyday I was in a bad mood when I arrived at my studio. I then analysed the content of the news and it was horrifying. Every morning I was fed with an economic note of depression, one politician calling another politician a liar and a cheat. I was fed with news of wars around the world and news of violence around the country. I was then given the weather report which further depressed me. If journalists presented a more accurate balanced view of the news, covering new discoveries, wonderful new inventions, positive images of people and nations we would find ourselves living in a paradise, not hell.'

I think it would help if we had politicians who were more light-hearted. Since the May 1997 General Election a lightness seems to have descended on the UK. Can this all be attributed to the charismatic Tony Blair? What will happen a year from now?

Everyone who holds a position in which they can influence others has a responsibility for creating an environment in which light-heartedness, fun and humour have a central place, even when the going is tough.

It is so easy to get work out of perspective and to become obsessive about it; it is also easy to hate work and resent the time it takes up. Bearing in mind we might spend over half our lives at work, and the majority of the rest of the time asleep, it's worth trying to make work fun and enjoyable. There is no reason to be masochistic. Laughter is a great stress-reliever and a manager's role should surely include responsibility for creating an environment which both fosters and supports healthy fun and laughter. This excludes cruel, ribald and discriminatory humour made at other people's expense.

The broadcaster Jenni Murray, also identified as charismatic in my survey, presents BBC Radio 4's *Woman's Hour*, and was invited to make the keynote speech at the European Women of Achievement Awards in 1994. Her speech was extremely successful; she told a very funny story about a visit she made to an airline where she met one of the aircraft crews. They explained with great pride that the cabin crew were all women and, very unusually, the flight crew were also women. She asked if she could visit the cockpit but was very politely told that they didn't have any use for one of those on the aircraft! Her timing was excellent and the humour perfect for the occasion.

> 'When I lived in Singapore I was trained by Jessie Owen. He had a world scholarship and trained the Singapore Schoolboys Relay Team. I was overawed by the man. He was a big man and commanded respect. He was absolutely outstanding; brought humour into it. Jessie Owen had real charisma, he made that relay team work.'
>
> *Paul Lever*

Entertainment

All the charismatic people I interviewed felt that they should be entertaining whenever appropriate. They wanted to enjoy interacting with others and, more importantly, they wanted to be engaging. It was important to them that people should want to listen to them, to enjoy the experience. Actors, first and foremost, must be entertaining: we are all actors and acting is like having charisma. Each is an interactive process. There are no actors without audiences and there are no charismatics without followers.

Actors who are not entertaining lose their audiences. So – all managers and leaders must be entertaining! Rather convoluted, but it makes the point. But how many of us try to be lively, pleasing and entertaining as we go about our work?

THE GREAT COMMUNICATORS – THROUGH ORATORY AND EXAMPLE

Martin Luther King, Hitler, Mussolini, Churchill, Arthur Scargill, Desmond Tutu, Mohammed, Jesus Christ, Billy Graham, Tom Peters ... and so the list goes on. We remember them not just for what they said but for how they said it. Not just what they wrote, not what they painted, not what they played, but the impact of their oratory. However, it is possible to be charismatic without being a brilliant orator. Neither Mother Theresa nor Gandhi would have won a public speaking competition. Their charisma is made obvious by their achievements far more than by their powers of oratory. Gandhi brought Britain to its knees through his campaign of non-violence and Mother Theresa won the Nobel Peace Prize by caring for paupers dying on the streets of Calcutta. Both illustrate the power of brilliant communication, but not oratory. They communicated through example, through their courage, persistence, energy, enthusiasm for their cause, and their spirituality and vision. Churchill was not a natural orator and he spent a lot of time perfecting his speeches. He left nothing to chance; he cultivated his serious 'bulldog' image in front of the mirror, for example. He often learned his speeches by heart and is known to have written one out carefully beforehand. He was a real craftsman.

Becoming a good speaker is within the capacity of us all, providing we want to develop this skill; and some have the potential to become brilliant. Each person's style of speaking is their own and we should aim to learn from, not copy, the masters. What are their secrets?

Winston Churchill	• Words that inspired and suited the moment – timing • Gravitas • Quality of voice • Wit • His position
Arthur Scargill	• Passion for his cause • Energy • Identification with his followers
Billy Graham	• Faith and passion • Empathy with audience • Enthusiasm
Martin Luther King	• Identification with the audience and the cause • Poetic language • Passion
Tony Blair	• Confidence • Personal image • Language • Energy
Heather Rabbatts	• Focus on the audience • Energy and enthusiasm • Personal integrity • Spontaneity
Margaret Thatcher	• Powerful and influential • Knowledge and command of subject • Conviction and passion • Achievements
Jenni Murray	• Friendly style of delivery • Humour • Modesty • Well researched • Popular

Looking at the descriptions above, how do you think people would describe your style of presentation or oratory? What makes your presentations memorable?

'There can be no question whatever that Mountbatten was a very charismatic leader. But he was an outstandingly unsuccessful junior officer in the navy. All his ships got into trouble and so on. He was also very largely unsuccessful when he was involved in combined operations. When he went to the Far East he went at precisely the right moment in the same way that Montgomery went to the Eighth army in the desert at the right moment, just when it was possible for things to turn. But you couldn't find a more charismatic leader than Mountbatten. He was something of an actor who communicated brilliantly and could speak the language of the people he was speaking to. You couldn't imagine a man more different to Montgomery. Montgomery inspired people by the way he spoke. He was a man who knew he was right, and who thought that he was more intelligent and able than anybody else. He inspired confidence for that reason. Mountbatten on the other hand inspired confidence because of his immense enthusiasm, his apparent willingness and ability to understand the difficulties that other people were going through, coupled with the fact that he was always there to make sure that they got what they needed.'

Sir John Acland

FAIL TO PREPARE? PREPARE TO FAIL!

Some people are natural presenters. Heather Rabbatts and Baroness Pitkeathley are much sought-after as speakers. Both have the power to enthral their audiences with very little preparation. Others need to learn the craft. And it is a craft – the craft of acting. Voice classes and acting courses are good investments for all of us. There is always something new to learn. It may be a way of enhancing our strengths, or developing a new style to try on appropriate occasions. Baroness Pitkeathley and Heather Rabbatts share some of their thoughts:

'I make a lot of speeches, that's the job. Sometimes in the season I make ten speeches a week, I had to learn to do that well. I'm irritated beyond measure by people who have to make a lot of speeches and never learn to do it well. I just think that's disrespectful to the audience. I also thinks it's disrespectful to make the same speech all the time. Being a good public speaker requires quite a lot of charisma because you engage with your audience, you want to feel that they'll warm to you, you want to have a joke with them, you want to challenge them but not to confront them. I believe that you need to be challenging in quite a gentle way ... I try to tease them a bit and maybe send them up a little rather than attack them.'

Baroness Pitkeathley

Heather Rabbatts is an exception.

'Even at a conference when I'm talking to 300 people, I never prepare, I never have anything written down; everybody else stands up with slides and projectors; I never have anything and there's a part of me that thinks one day I'm going to stand up and have nothing to say – this could be a problem!'

Heather Rabbatts

LAST WORD

If I could choose to have only one of the charismatic keys it would be this one – the ability to *communicate* effectively. I'd want to have passion and enthusiasm. I'd want to be known as a person who expressed their feelings, who showed that they cared and as someone who was fun to be with. These are the qualities which help people share visions and intentions, collect and disseminate information, lead, manage, love, and care.

SUMMARY

- The ability to communicate effectively is a vital skill for managers and leaders
- Communication means imparting information and evoking understanding
- Communication is a two-way process – the communicator and the receiver must be engaged
- Charismatic communication involves the ability to inspire, passion, feelings, emotion and enthusiasm
- Charismatic communication is *electric*
- Language and voice *must* reflect feelings
- We are all actors and must learn our craft
- Personal presence – our inner body image – projects personal energy and confidence
- Image makes a substantial contribution to the message
- Humour, used with care, enhances communication
- Presentations should be carefully planned and rehearsed.

Action points

- Communicate with passion, feelings, enthusiasm and emotion
- Develop the ability to use your sixth sense – your ISP
- Recognise and project your chosen image
- Use humour with care
- Develop excellent presentation skills.

YOU'VE GOT TO HAVE STYLE ...

1. If you turned up to a party either over- or under-dressed would you
    - (a) go home to change ☐
    - (b) keep a low profile all evening ☐
    - (c) forget it and enjoy yourself? ☐

2. Do you leave the generation of ideas to others?
    - (a) yes, other people are much better at it
      than I so I leave them to it ☐
    - (b) no, I always try to contribute something ☐

3. How much time do you spend every week playing?
    - (a) I do not play ☐
    - (b) at least an hour ☐
    - (c) too many! ☐

4. How many role models do you have?
    - (a) one ☐
    - (b) two or more ☐
    - (c) none ☐

5. Are you in love with your work?
    - (a) yes ☐
    - (b) no ☐
    - (c) I do not understand the question ☐

6. How many of Edward de Bono's books have you read?
    - (a) at least half a dozen ☐
    - (b) one ☐
    - (c) none ☐
    - (d) none, but I have read other books on creativity ☐

7. People say that I have style
    - (a) frequently ☐
    - (b) sometimes ☐
    - (c) never ☐

8. Style just means the clothes that people wear
    - (a) I agree ☐
    - (b) I disagree ☐

9. When did you last recognise that you learned something?
    - (a) on a training programme some time ago ☐
    - (b) last week ☐

(c) I haven't learned anything for a very long time ☐

(d) I consciously learn all the time ☐

10. Do you think that you are curious?
(a) no ☐
(b) yes ☐
(c) yes, very curious ☐

11. Which one of these people do you think has the most style?
(a) Diana, Princess of Wales ☐
(b) Placido Domingo ☐
(c) André Agassi ☐
(e) none of them ☐

Score

1. (a) 0	2. (a) 1	3. (a) 0	4. (a) 1	5. (a) 5	6. (a) 3
(b) 2	(b) 5	(b) 2	(b) 5	(b) 2	(b) 5
(c) 5		(c) 10	(c) −1	(c) 0	(c) 0
					(d) 5

7. (a) 5	8. (a) 0	9. (a) 1	10. (a) 0	11. (a) 5
(b) 3	(b) 5	(b) 3	(b) 3	(b) 5
(c) 0		(c) 0	(c) 5	(c) 5
		(d) 5		(d) 0

Score ☐

Total available: 60 marks. If you scored

➤ Over 55   You *definitely* have real style.

➤ Between 40 and 55   You are an original and independent person with style.

➤ Between 30 and 40   You are missing a lot in life. Let go, and try to be less inhibited.

➤ Under 30   You are taking life much too seriously. Try to take few more risks in your thinking and doing. Discuss how you can do this with a friend.

Key 4 THE STYLE KEY

'To live is not just to survive, but to thrive with passion, compassion, some humour and style.'

Maya Angelou

In 1967, sodden and footsore, I found myself taking part in the British School Girls' expedition to the wet, windy and glorious Faroe Islands. Nineteen young women mapped the terrain, ate puffins and generally did other exploring-type things. The weather was not kind to us; rain fell in sheets, the river flooded and drowned our campsite, and the seas between the islands were rough. Wet and tired, we struggled over never-ending volcanic ridges, carrying between 40–60 pounds of very basic kit (nothing lightweight in those days). We lived on 'Surprise Peas', dried egg, chocolate and potatoes. Oh, the character-building that went on for some of us! But every morning, one of our number emerged from her tent in rollers and pink baby doll pyjamas barely concealed under her anorak. Now *she had style*. She was really different.

Style describes the way we do things, the way we do anything: our way of dressing, managing people and speaking; the kinds of possessions we have; and the way we conduct ourselves. When our way of doing things is different – and superior – then we are said to have *style*. She of the rollers and pink pyjamas had style. She was different in her pursuit of excellence, wanting to make the best of herself under very difficult conditions. She realised that style and excellence are not put on for other people. The rest of us poor souls did not. Style reflects qualities that matter to ourselves. Sir Antony Acland was full of admiration for the way in which Lady Thatcher always appeared perfectly groomed even on the most uncomfortable of tours. (There is no doubt about it, men do have it easier!) Those with real style are *authentic*. Everything about them is real and it makes them stand out from the crowd – they are the 'real thing'. Charismatic individuals are all exceptionally distinctive. Heather Rabbatts' love of flamboyant clothes and jewellery is not something she puts on for work. She dresses for herself to reflect her personality.

> 'Somebody wrote on a lavatory wall: "Paul Lever, how to succeed without trying". The reason for that was my style. I've always brought humour into it.'
>
> *Paul Lever*

I talked to Lieutenant General Mike Jackson about his style. I had asked to see him because Edwina Currie identified him as charismatic. She felt he was very flamboyant, and had real style. I asked him if he was able to be more flamboyant in the field than in a staff role:

'I don't know if I would wish to be described as flamboyant. It has a slight connotation of personal indulgence about it! Perhaps without much intellectual backing!

My military hero is the Duke of Wellington. He had enormous competence, and great personal style in a slightly aesthetic way. His handling of other people was absolutely brilliant; he was very witty. And yet in himself, he appears to have been devoid of bombast, with a complete lack of pomposity in his style, dress and his behaviour. He didn't need outward props. Napoleon, on the other hand, was bombastic, did need appurtenances and pomposities to sort of bolster himself up. And he lost, didn't he! A light-hearted story of Wellington shows his real style. During the Peninsular War when people went on leave to Lisbon, a certain officer on the Duke's Staff was late back, so he was wheeled in front of the great man: "Why were you absent?" Out comes this heart-rending story of this wonderful senorita. Clearly we are dealing with passion. "That's quite enough of all that – 72 hours in bed with the same woman is quite enough for any man. You are fined one hundred pounds." Another anecdote gives a poignant view of life before Waterloo. "My Lord, do we prevail tomorrow?" "I've no idea, it all depends on that object", pointing to a private soldier, picking his nose. Absolutely brilliant!'

Sir Antony Acland feels that his brother Major General Sir John Acland has a very charismatic style of leadership, particularly evident when he was in Rhodesia. He described his brother as having a mixture of flamboyance and strong character: rushing about, sometimes looking like a 'proper' Major General in the Scots Guards and sometimes looking like a sort of guerrilla leader, wearing red socks and a jungle hat.

Successful military men seem to have an abundance of style.

LOTS MORE DIFFERENCE

'It's not what I do but how I do it.
It's not what I say but how I say it
And how I look when I am saying and doing it.'
Mae West

Difference is the defining factor. Style requires us to be different, to stand out from the crowd, and that is never easy. On the whole, human beings like doing things together, behaving in a similar fashion, believing the same things and having the same possessions. We can be very suspicious of new ideas and people who are different. This is easy to see on both a global and a local scale, where people of different ethnic and religious backgrounds and behaviours are often regarded with great suspicion. If this suspicion cannot be overcome, serious conflict can arise.

Keeping up with the Joneses is another way of ensuring solidarity. We do not want people to be different, to have things that we haven't. Most children want to be the same as their peers. Parents often forget that being different can be extraordinarily painful for their children. Small things like having to wear a handknitted pullover when everyone else in the class has a shop-bought one can feel like the end of the world. There is nothing *wrong* in wanting to be the same, in not wanting to be different. But don't expect to be a trend-setter. If you're going to be a follower, be a good follower.

COURAGE UNDER FIRE

'If all else fails, fame can always be assured by spectacular error.'
J K Galbraith

Remember Eddie the Eagle? That man had real style. Anyone who can launch themselves down a steep ramp 300 feet high, reach a speed of over 60 mph, jump into space standing on a couple of boards and expect to land safely is pushing their luck anyway, but to do that with very little training, in borrowed kit, and knowing that you have no real chance of success, says something about you. Mad, yes – but more than that. Eddie the Eagle had a dream – to be a ski jumper no matter what. He had amazing physical courage and he had *style*. That was his way of doing things. Being different requires courage. True, the rewards can be great – success, adulation, admiration, respect, and fame. But the price can be high – isolation, misunderstanding, misrepresentation, failure, ignominy, pity, jealousy, and antagonism. Remember how Sir Clive Sinclair was ridiculed for his baby car concept? And yet, in today's environmentally aware climate, it's just the thing! An idea before its time.

'On the wider stage, great visionary leaders have the courage to abandon old ideas and do things differently. Nelson Mandela had the courage to become a unifying president. It would have been far more understandable for him to portray himself as an embittered vengeful leader determined to get his own back on a regime that imprisoned him for 27 years. Jesus Christ had the courage to challenge traditional Jewish thought and practice. Edwina Currie and Clare Short have had the courage to tell people what they really think despite official party thinking. For Jean-Marie Descarpentries, courage is certainly important:

> 'One of the most important qualities of charisma for me is courage, you have to be courageous; always take difficult decisions not only for you, but for your company.'

The question has to be – is the price worth paying?

Charismatic individuals are people who *are* prepared to pay the price for being different. Sometimes things go well, sometimes they don't – but they remain committed to doing things their way. Difference is one of the defining characteristics of charisma. Benedict Allen knows he is different, and he puts this down to his style of doing things:

> 'I certainly have a style of doing things which is almost unique, probably for very good reasons. I've had to find my own path, and despite the world really rather than because of it, I've managed to find my goal, my dream. I remember a very distinguished explorer saying in *The Telegraph*, "Oh well, dear old Benedict" and dismissed me. Exploration is full of egos and it's a good competitive world like any other field. A lot of that feeling of "you don't fit the normal rules, you're not a scientist, you're not a serious explorer". I have been knocked a lot but the support of my parents and a growing circle of friends supported me in finding my own way of doing things.'

Edwina Currie described Lady Thatcher's style:

'She gave a lot of attention to her appearance. She was striking looking. She got better and better, she had super legs and made sure everybody saw them. She would bat her eyelashes in a most unnerving way. Women loved it because they could see what she was up to and the men just fell about. She was only 49 when she was elected and she was a very good-looking woman; she still is in some ways.'

Being different can be very frightening indeed. Quite unconsciously and automatically our stomachs tense up, our hearts race and the blood drains from our faces to our legs, ready for 'fight or flight'. One of the best ways of coping with fear is to smile – consciously. It is difficult to smile and experience intense fear at the same time because the processes are very different. Smiling requires that we relax our face muscles, especially those round the eyes and mouth, whereas fear is about tension, preparing us to run from whatever.

Even important people can find some experiences frightening. Sir Antony Acland describes giving the eulogy for Sir Alec Douglas Hume in Westminster Abbey at which 2500 people and members of the Royal Family were to be present. He described this as one of the most awe-inspiring, frightening thing he has ever done. When I asked him if he normally gets anxious before public presentations he said, yes, everyone should get anxious. If they aren't anxious, they lose something. He remembers Lady Thatcher being anxious to get it right before speaking to the boys at Eton. She admitted being nervous about speaking to a young audience, all under 18. Hope for us all I think.

> *Innovate* – bring in novelties, make changes.
> *Create* – bring into existence, give rise to.
> *Concise Oxford Dictionary*

Style is about flair, éclat and élan. It requires *creativity* of mind. Gertrude Shilling's Ascot hats, Anita Roddick's Body Shop, Stephen Spielberg's films and NASA's spacecraft are all products of creative minds. Unfortunately, creativity is not a highly rated quality within the world of management, if we are to believe the findings of Ned Herrmann. In 1995 he surveyed 773 managers in six countries: England, the United States, Germany, France, Australia and Turkey. They were asked to rate 16 work elements in order of importance, including 'creative aspects' and 'innovation'. Innovation was more highly rated than creativity, which Herrmann finds unfortunate. There was little difference in the ratings of men and women managers. Herrmann believes that creativity, representing knowledge outside the business, is just as important, if not more, than innovation, which essentially looks at doing the same things in new ways. Creativity is about doing very different things. 'Creative aspects' was rated thirteenth by English managers, compared with fourth by their Australian counterparts. Dr Harry Alder's study of 150 UK business leaders is a little more encouraging in that all those he interviewed identified creativity as a major factor in their success.

We must be prepared to use all the potential we have, which means allowing both sides of our brains to develop. The right side of our brain appears to be responsible for intuition and creative thought and the left for more logical and analytical thinking. Management has traditionally valued left-brain activities far more than those of the right, with the result that there is often little appreciation of the potential available to organisations which lies within the heads of each and every employee. The emergence of the 'learning organisation' has brought the issue into much clearer focus and it is to be hoped that 'creativity' will soon reach the top of the list of qualities to be developed and encouraged. Obviously, there are ways that each one of us can develop this aspect.

THE MOUSE

Walt Disney, surely one of the most creative individuals this century, devised a system to assist his creative process. First of all he created his dream or vision of the whole film. Then he looked at his plan realistically. He gathered all the necessary information to make sure that his dream could become a reality. He balanced money, time, and resources against this dream. Finally, he took another look from the point of view of a critical member of the audience. Disney used three different processes: the Dreamer; the Realist; and the Critic.

Evelyn Glennie does it in a different way:

'In the work that I do I haven't had a role model to learn from. So in a way I've had to experiment with all aspects, the playing itself, the constructing of the programme, what I wear, how I present myself, all these kind of things. I think a lot about style but I've had to experiment – a lot hasn't worked and a lot has worked. I possibly think more about style than anything.'

'Dans le champs d'observation, l'hasard ne favorise que les esprits préparés.'

Louis Pasteur

When we think of ideas, we tend to think that all ideas have to be good ones. They don't. *What is important is letting ourselves have the ideas in the first place*: letting our right brains out of the strait-jacket so easily imposed by the left, our rational logical self. Creativity is about playing with 'building blocks' of information and knowledge, putting them down in unfamiliar patterns. Children are naturally creative thinkers and we adults have to recapture the curiosity and creativity of childhood if we are to maximise our potential for creativity.

Louis Pasteur said that 'chance favours the prepared mind'. Creativity is not a chance activity. It requires hard work – putting the pieces of information and knowledge on the shelves ready to pull off when the opportunity occurs. No building blocks, no creative idea. And where does the knowledge and information come from? Curiosity. Finding out. Learning. Children learn through play; they work hard at it.

Great ideas are usually the result of our building on the ideas of others. Tony Buzan described how this is done:

'Einstein didn't buck the system, Da Vinci didn't buck the system; they actually took all the gems of knowledge that the system had, amalgamated them into their own knowledge base and then with that knowledge, leapt into the next paradigm of genius thought. Creativity is not antagonistic, it is entirely cooperative. A better metaphor is like mountain climbers on ropes. The one who is at the top is the leader of the climb; very often that person will take the last place after a while. Similarly, when people are skiing across a long expanse, one will take the lead for a while until another member of the team assumes the leadership role. So it's a cooperative venture with the past and with the present and into the future.'

ARE YOU A SUPERBABY?

Tony Buzan, describes the vital elements of play as curiosity, synaesthesia (the blending of senses, a multisensory capacity where colour is equated with sound, rhythm with shape, taste with touch and sight with feeling), enjoyment, openness and wonder, serious intention, passion and involvement, repetition and practice, relaxed concentration and unconditional self-acceptance. He believes that it is possible for adults to learn faster than babies by becoming a *superbaby*, by combining 'babylike playfulness with your adult cognitive skills and resources'. Surprising as it may seem, these words – curiosity, enjoyment, openness and wonder, serious intention, passion and involvement, repetition and practice, relaxed concentration and unconditional self-acceptance – are all words I would associate with charismatic individuals! How would you rate yourself on all those words? Are you a *superbaby*?

Fred Dibnah described how he achieved one of his life's goals by being creative:

'One day I was mending the baths' chimney and a head popped up over the top of the roof and said, "I'm from the engineers department at Bolton Council, we've a problem with the town hall clock". He said that the stone pillars had badly eroded and they were going to fall out. They'd had this estimate from some modernistic outfit called Synthetic Resin Bonded Stone Dust – in other words, concrete made in a mould. Well, that was like an insult to our town hall. "I'm sure that I could find an answer, turn some stones, etc." So I had all sorts of weird ideas and I asked to go and have a look. We went armed with dividers and compasses and sheets of cardboard and scissors and made a collection of templates. We made a new pillar and then got the contract to do 18 of them, which at that time in my life – I was nearly 25 – was my ultimate goal in life: to have actually mended the town hall clock in Bolton!'

'What is this life if, full of care
We have no time to stand and stare?'

W H Davies

I suspect that many people will have had the experience of worrying through a problem, sleeping on it and – lo and behold – a creative response pops up in the morning. We need to give ourselves time to 'stand and stare'. Much good and creative work can be done on the golf course, in the bar, at the health club or even just walking the dog. Creative work does not have to be done 'at work', within the confines of the office walls. We have to get used to the idea that what is required of us is an outcome. That's what we have to deliver – our *presence* at work is not enough in itself. As managers we need to ensure that we understand this in relation to those we supervise. The workplace is rarely the best place in which to generate new ideas.

WHY DO WE LOSE OUR CURIOSITY AND CREATIVITY?

'He asked his broad aunt, the Hippopotamus, why her eyes were red, and his broad aunt, the Hippopotamus, spanked him with her broad, broad hoof; and he asked his hairy uncle the Baboon, why melons tasted just so, and his hairy uncle the Baboon, spanked him with his hairy, hairy paw. And still he was full of 'satiable curiosity! He asked questions about everything that he saw, or heard, or felt, or touched, and all his uncles and his aunts spanked him. And still he was full of 'satiable curiosity!'

Rudyard Kipling, The Elephant's Child

Parents are keen to have conforming children. 'Way out' thinking is different and as we know difference is difficult to tolerate. Tony Buzan describes an experience he had on the Tube one day. He

'... was sitting just behind a five-year-old girl and her mother. The train was accelerating well beyond the normal speed for underground trains, and the little girl, becoming excited, exclaimed to her mother, "Mummy, wouldn't it be amazing if this train could keep going faster, until it was going so fast it could take us into tomorrow? We could then go home and tell Daddy what was going to happen in the future!" The mother yelled, "Don't ever say such a stupid thing again".'

This is not an isolated example. It happens everyday, everywhere. And we wonder why we lose so much of our creativity and curiosity!

The child was displaying extraordinary insight, playing with ideas in the same way that Einstein did when he formulated his theory of relativity. He imagined himself on an accelerating sunbeam! Daniel Goleman's book *Emotional Intelligence* is a very good read for parents who would like more guidance on encouraging creativity in their children.

Little extra

I asked Evelyn Glennie, what is the little 'something else' that she puts into her performances?

> 'I don't know, I think it's a feeling of danger, something that hasn't been worked out or prepared in the rehearsal room. I think it's a feeling – you just decide you're going to experiment on the platform. I seem to do a lot of this. It seems to suit my kind of character. I can take the score and learn the rules within the privacy of my four walls and then once I'm on the platform I just break the rules. So it gives the audience a feeling that they aren't quite sure of what's going to come up next.'

MANAGERIAL OLYMPICS

Style is about excellence. It's about being 'superior'. It's about being better than others at something – and why not? Daley Thompson's *raison d'être* was to be the best at something; the best decathlete in the world. And he was, with two Olympic gold medals to prove it. The decathlon has much to teach us. As we have seen in previous chapters, managers are the decathletes of the world of work. Our 'event' requires us to compete in a number of areas including the management of people, technical processes and specialist functions; in financial management and commercial understanding; strategic and operational thinking and planning, to name but a few. We should strive for excellence in our areas of strength. We should encourage others to strive for excellence in their areas of strength and, if our strengths lie in managing people, we should manage people; if in selling, we should sell; if in teaching, we should teach. Unfortunately, when we demonstrate strength and excellence in one area, we are often promoted into a position where we are unable to perform as effectively. As the Peter Principle implies, we are promoted above our level of competence. However, this does not mean we should not try to learn new skills.

Managers achieve and learn best when they are working on issues that interest and concern them most, rather than on unrelated theoretical concepts. That is why management development programmes using the principles of action learning – that is, using issues of interest and concern to the participants as the main vehicle for learning – can achieve such a good return on investment.

'… to make my worst better than anyone else's best.'

Daley Thompson

'The heart of man does not tolerate the absence of the excellent and supreme.'

Jose Ortega y Gasset, Meditations on Quixot

HOW DO WE ACHIEVE EXCELLENCE?

This can be more difficult for those of us who do not enter races or perform in a more formal way. How do we become excellent at what we do? First of all, we have to *want to be excellent* at what we do. It has been rather fashionable over the last 25 years or so to be very blasé about what we do at work. We did enough to get by and only a few people really exerted themselves. However, the last few years have seen a major change as organisations restructure and jobs become less secure and management roles disappear. How many of us could really put hand on heart and say that we are really motivated to want to become 'excellent' to the point where we could match Daley Thompson's aim 'to make his worst better than anyone else's best'? To be a better marketing manager than anyone else, a better general manager, a better speaker? If we had such ambitions we would have goals and objectives to work towards. To do this, we need a strategy: how am I going to get there?

One way is to observe and study excellence in the area in which we want to succeed. Identify, and then study, an expert. Observe in two ways: first, analyse the technical elements of the expert's performance. What is it that they do well? What don't they do at all? We can learn as much from what experts don't do as what they do do. Secondly, be receptive. Be open to the whole experience. What must it be like to do something so effortlessly, for effortlessness is the hallmark of excellence? Try and *feel* what it would be like, *visualise* what it would be like. Put yourself in your expert's place. How would it feel to close a multimillion pound sale? How would it feel to implement a new organisational structure successfully? What would opening a new factory be like?

Those committed to achieving excellence are dedicated to continuous learning and achieving high standards in all they do, disciplining themselves unmercifully. They are masters of persistence and perseverance, while at the same time enjoying what they do. They are in love with what they do. Evelyn Glennie talked passionately about excellence:

'It's the one thing that probably keeps me going. I am never satisfied. As soon as I walk off the platform I immediately analyse everything to death. It's just a kind of horrible little period that I go through after every single concert. Then I wake up the next morning and somehow go back to the drawing board and start again. That's why I find it difficult when people say – oh, you play wonderfully – I'm very happy they think that but actually I feel like drowning myself or something! I can never really stand back from what I do because I am too much involved with it. Yes, I practise but I feel as though I'm a student all the time. With percussion it is particularly true because it's played such an important part in so many different cultures; I am literally a student … when I see a new instrument, wow what do I do with that? In a way it's probably why I didn't get on so well with the educational system. I didn't like being part of a system. I find that I have to explore things in my own way and so I've never really been the sort of individual who likes to have a teacher for a number of years. I just have to explore something myself.'

Excellence applies in every area of our lives. We must become students of excellence and look for models of excellence wherever we can. Tony Buzan felt that we all wanted to be the best at something:

'Everybody who sees the best, the best runner, the best skater, the best dancer – wants to be able to mimic that or peform to a similar standard of excellence. This could be described as jealousy – a positive jealousy. We all want to be like the best which is a beautiful, elegant and sophisticated survival mechanism. We *should* want to be like the best – it is our ultimate survival mechanism.'

THEY ARE IN LOVE …

'Charisma has to be about how other people react to you. I think some of that has to be about passion, commitment and conviction as well. I also think it probably has to be something around loving what you do. I've been doing this job nearly ten years now and in two years we'll be celebrating our tenth anniversary. It's not been easy; there have been times when it's been very hard. But I can honestly tell you that every morning, or virtually every morning, I wake up excited about what I'm going to do at work that day – even if it is going to see the new minister and thinking 'oh Christ!', I am excited and stimulated by it.'

Baroness Pitkeathley

There is nothing wrong with being in love with work. Nothing at all. Being in love means passion, enthusiasm and excitement – and fun! But, as in our personal lives, we should not be in love with something to the exclusion of all else. I meet many managers at all levels in the course of my work in management development, and I am always deeply saddened when I meet managers who devote almost all their waking hours to their work. They are rarely at home. They miss their children growing up and lose touch with their wives (they are mostly men). Unfortunately, such dedication is *not* a drive for excellence. Younger managers often do this because they feel obliged to live up to the prevailing macho corporate culture which measures commitment and effectiveness in terms of hours spent at work. Desperate! Sometimes it's because they feel that they have to be seen to put in more hours than anyone else; sometimes they feel that they have to match the hours put in by more senior managers. But serving time, for this is what it amounts to, belongs in prisons and nowhere else. In older managers it tends to be the result of a mistaken idea that they are indispensable. Both are examples of macho management.

Achieving a balance between work, home and self is vital. I find women much better at achieving a balance between the first two, normally because they have to. But they are woefully poor at spending any time on themselves. In today's world we have to work smarter, not harder. Of course, there are times when we all have to put in long hours, but doing this day in and day out is counter-productive. Looking after the needs of self is the most important of the three. Looking after self ensures that we will be in a fit state to do the other two. Unfortunately, many people find it difficult to justify spending time on themselves. This attitude needs to be challenged and changed.

ARE YOU ONE IN A MILLION?

Charismatics are not like anyone else. They do not behave like other people – in their bearing, self-confidence, possessions, what they are prepared to say, or what they actually say. They are not clones, not even of other charismatics. Charismatics are one in a million. Charismatics use their instincts all the time. Instinct allows them to behave without conscious thought; they use unconscious skills and instinctive impulse.

A REAL COMPLIMENT

Which would you rather have said about you?

- 'You are very energetic'
- 'She has a great deal of courage'
- 'You have real style'
- 'He is a brilliant communicator'
- 'You really know how to make things happen'

For me it has to be the third one. I would be thrilled with any of those comments, but if anyone says I have style – that is a *real* compliment! Style is personal. It is impossible to copy. It is the one quality that distinguishes one person from another because it is unique – the way that person does something. Only *they* do it that way. And it is not an accolade that people award lightly, which makes it all the more worth having. All the people I met had style in abundance – their own very individual ways of doing things, which I found very inspiring. Among this elite company two of them in particular stand out for me – Fred Dibnah and Evelyn Glennie. Both of them had a special magic for me. They both radiated joy in what they do and a delight in doing things in their own particular way. They both pursue excellence with incredible enthusiasm and both are lifelong learners. They are both persistent in the extreme and their commitment is extraordinary.

Style is fun, it is different, it is personal and it is very well worth having.

Can we learn it? We can develop it, and I suspect that it is developed over time. Develop confidence, add a big dash of courage and a hefty sprinkling of creativity, and it would be difficult not to have style. Charismatics are out of the ordinary. They have flair – a selective instinct for what is excellent. *Charismatics have style*. Work at developing your own style with pride and enthusiasm.

SUMMARY

- Style describes the way we do things
- Style is about excellence and superiority of achievement
- Style requires the courage to be different
- Curiosity and creativity are the basis of style
- Creativity is a right-brain activity
- The drive for excellence lies within us all.

Action points

- Develop curiosity
- Learn to play again
- Become a 'Superbaby'
- Train as a managerial decathlete
- Observe style and excellence and learn from examples
- Develop a passion for learning
- Feel and visualise
- Love what you do
- Be courageous
- Develop your own style with pride.

ARE YOU A MOVER AND SHAKER? DO YOU MAKE THINGS HAPPEN?

1. Even when I am very busy, people ask me to do things because they know I will get them done
    (a) always ☐
    (b) sometimes ☐
    (c) they know I do not get things done ☐

2. I dream about achieving great things
    (a) never ☐
    (b) often ☐
    (c) occasionally ☐
    (d) I do not dream ☐

3. Once I have decided to do something
    (a) I do not give up ☐
    (b) I can easily change my mind ☐
    (c) it depends ... ☐

4. I would rather do something myself to ensure that it is done properly, than give it to someone else to do
    (a) always ☐
    (b) usually ☐
    (c) not necessarily ☐

5. People choose to have me in their team because they think I am a good team member
    (a) yes ☐
    (b) sometimes ☐
    (c) people don't think I am a good team member ☐

6. I understand the differences between leadership and management
    (a) yes ☐
    (b) not really ☐

7. I am easily distracted
    (a) yes ☐
    (b) no, I am very single-minded ☐
    (c) only when I want to be ☐

8. Everything I do sets a good example to others
    (a) true ☐
    (b) sometimes true ☐
    (c) never true ☐

9. I prefer to achieve things
    (a) on my own ☐

    (b) as part of a team   ☐

    (c) I am equally happy to work in both ways   ☐

10. Once I start a project
    (a) I always get it finished   ☐
    (b) I sometimes get it finished   ☐
    (c) it may never get finished unless I have help
        from someone else   ☐

11. 'Energetic' describes me
    (a) well   ☐
    (b) some of the time   ☐
    (c) inaccurately!   ☐

Score

1. (a) 10	2. (a) 0	3. (a) 5	4. (a) 1	5. (a) 5	6. (a) 5
(b) 5	(b) 5	(b) 0	(b) 2	(b) 3	(b) 0
(c) 0	(b) 3	(c) 2	(c) 5	(c) 1	
	(b) –1				

7. (a) 1	8. (a) 5	9. (a) 0	10. (a) 5	11. (a) 5
(b) 4	(b) 2	(b) 0	(b) 2	(b) 3
(c) 5	(b) 0	(c) 5	(c) 0	(c) 0

Score ☐

Total available: 60 marks. If you scored:

- Over 55   You are one of life's movers and shakers.
- Between 40 and 55   You are pretty reliable and do not let the grass grow under your feet.
- Between 30 and 40   You might find it helpful to explore ways of getting things done.
- Under 30   Life must be very hard. Discuss how you could become more effective at getting things done with a friend.

Key 5 THE MOVING AND SHAKING KEY

'I longed really for my dreams and nothing else. People used to think of me as a "dreamy little boy" and some say I'm quite vague; but I certainly snap into action quite a lot more in the forest, because that is my world. But those dreams have helped me through, they've lifted me up, taken me over barriers. It always surprises people that I pull these things off.'

Benedict Allen

Jeffrey Archer, now Lord Archer, is another *mover and shaker*. He makes things happen. There aren't many people who make a fortune, lose it, and then make another, larger, one in a relatively short time. He chose to do it by moving into a new area for him. He moved from politician to popular novelist. When asked how he did this, he explained his 'kings, princes and paupers' idea: 'We don't lack talent, we lack energy.' And of course, he is right. Human beings have incredible potential, which few of us even try to maximise. Those who have energy and talent, but particularly energy, like Lord Archer, do very well!

Lady Thatcher is renowned for her energy. Her ability to get by with very little sleep caused many of her colleagues real difficulties. She never stopped. Richard Branson is on the go all the time. Robert Maxwell, Fred Dibnah, Evelyn Glennie – the list is endless. They have reservoirs of energy which enable them to drive things forward all the time. Their drive is fuelled by passion for their goals and ambitions. One of my interviewees said:

'It's the buzz, the excitement of doing what you want to. The more I do, the more happens which then gives me more to do. Together with my team, we achieve the goals we set ourselves and more besides. And it's that very success that drives me on to the next thing. I love it. When everything is going really well, I don't want to stop. I get so much satisfaction from what I am doing. It's like being on a roller-coaster – fast-moving and very exciting, even though you know what is going to happen.'

Les Williams remembers Robert Maxwell having amazing drive:

'You and I might have a conversation, a casual chat and then we go away and do whatever. It was never like that with him. He always had to be driving for something, pushing and bullying or whatever.

People recognised his drive immediately: "this man is going to make a difference, he's going to do something now and if we keep our eye on him we might see what's going on." He really did have that, the ability to make things move.'

WHERE DOES ENERGY COME FROM?

Baroness Pitkeathley thinks that charisma is:

'... tied up with energy. It may not be energy in the way one thinks, although I do have a great deal of physical energy, it's something around the feeling of energy that people give out. I think it's about my energy because I don't give up, I do keep on. It's also about being fired and refired anew everyday, and I mean literally every day. It's about being reenergised all the time by that, by individuals and by the issue.'

Against the odds

There is another way of looking at it. There are three types of people: those who make things happen; those who watch what happened; and those who wonder what happened. *Movers and shakers* belong to the first group. Mrs Perween Warsi, managing director of S&A Foods in Derby, is one of the most outstanding *movers and shakers* I know personally. She was born and brought up in India in a traditional Muslim home and, although she enjoyed educational opportunities, she did not see herself as a career woman. In 1975 she married a doctor and moved to the UK with him; the next ten years saw her fulfilling the demanding role of doctor's wife and mother of two sons. Perween has always had a passion and flair for cooking and creating recipes. Encouraged by family and friends she turned this into a business, working from her own kitchen at home selling takeaway dishes to individuals and restaurants. Soon after launching, her recipes became very popular and within months the volume had increased substantially. In 1987 she won a contract to supply the supermarket chain Asda, and set up a factory to produce the food. Now, some ten years later, with a multiplicity of well-known supermarket customers all over Europe and a turnover of some £30 million, Michael Heseltine has opened her new factory which is one of the most advanced in Europe. Forging a successful career is difficult for most women. Achieving this in an adopted country, managing two cultures and traditions, looking after and encouraging her family, surviving the ups and downs of business, and continuing to lead her company from strength to strength in a highly competitive market place makes Perween Warsi an amazing woman: a real *mover and shaker*. She is a small, delightful, very attractive woman who oozes determination. When she makes a prediction you know it will happen. In 1997, against nominees from 35 countries, Perween was presented with the Life Achievement Award by the World Congress of Women Business Owners in Los Angeles: a lesson for us all.

Lieutenant General Mike Jackson agrees that movers and shakers generate their own opportunities:

> 'In some ways perhaps I may need the situation to bring out the best in me, as opposed to the real movers and shakers who are very clever at creating their own positions. They are more like entrepreneurs if you like, creating the business opportunities.'

For Evelyn Glennie age brings realisation:

> 'Making things happen, along with vision and strategy, is something that I'm very much aware of. The older I get the more I realise that I do have to "move and shake" and adapt and change in all aspects of what I do. This is probably the story of my life; I'm always changing, experimenting, and adapting because it's the only way to learn.'

WHAT IS IT THAT MOVERS AND SHAKERS *DO* TO MAKE THINGS HAPPEN?

They all start off with a dream, with a clear vision. Benedict Allen dreamt of being an explorer: Mother Theresa and Cynthia Homer both knew what God wanted them to do: Evelyn Glennie knew what she wanted to do in life, as did Fred Dibnah; Jill Pitkeathley knows what she wants to do with the Carers Association; Heather Rabbatts knows exactly what she wants to do at Lambeth Borough Council; Sir John Harvey Jones is very clear about his mission.

> 'I think I've always had vision and that has been probably one of my strong points. I've always known since I was I teenager what I've wanted to do, and I've gone for it. To be fairly accurate I've known since the age of 15. Once I'd decided that I wanted to be a solo percussionist then that was that and absolutely nothing got in the way. Even now with ideas and projects and things I really want to do, if I believe in them – then I just do it. That's quite handy because it means that I don't waste time – I get it done.'
>
> *Evelyn Glennie*

All the charismatic people I interviewed have one particular quality in abundance: they are all passionate about what they do. They talked enthusiastically about their work and their beliefs, sometimes quietly and sometimes in a very animated way. I felt their underlying energy and passion, expressed through their voices, their eyes and their whole body language.

They all radiate a very contagious enthusiasm. So, number one, *know* what you want to do and go for it with enthusiasm. This is the *Vision Key*.

However, if you are a perfectionist you might have a problem with getting started. Many people will not even contemplate beginning something unless they feel that it is going to be perfect from the outset. Unfortunately, perfection is rarely achieved immediately and consequently things don't get started. Striving to achieve perfection is fine once you get going, but the drive for perfection must never be allowed to impede progress. The focus must be on moving forward, working to achieve goals and ambitions. Think of it in military terms – advancing and capturing territory. But good commanders ensure that there are soldiers in the rear of the advance 'mopping up' as they go, working to ensure nothing goes wrong – achieving perfection, if you like. Companies are the same. They move into new markets; all the details have not been totally worked out and much of this will have to be done once things begin to happen; the important thing is getting a foothold. I learnt that personally from Gordon Wills. In the early days of the International Management Centres he insisted that we started management development programmes, even when I could think of many good reasons to delay. But, of course, he was right. IMC started with all its imperfections. If we hadn't made a start, there would have been nothing to improve. IMC has always been a learning organisation and we have learned and improved ourselves over time. And so it is with individuals. Perween Warsi's first kitchen wasn't perfect but it was a start.

Ready, Aim, Fire? No, no, no! *Fire, Aim, Ready!*

Try, try and try again …

'A learner driver took her first test after 1500 lessons – and failed for dangerous driving. Sue Evan-Jones has spent more than £18,000 over 26 years trying to get her licence. The mother of three failed her test because she slammed down on the clutch instead of the brake in an emergency stop. She also ploughed through roadworks and swerved into the middle of the road.'

'Learner Driver Taught Lesson', Telegraph and Argus

This lady certainly gets marks for persistence. Can you imagine – 26 YEARS?! OK, so she failed – but with determination like that she will pass one day.

Gordon Wills visited a prospective client 23 times before there was ever a hint of work. He secured a big contract in the end, but it took 18 months of nothing. Everyone told Evelyn Glennie that she couldn't possibly be a professional musician because she was profoundly deaf. Neither of them took no for an answer. Neither of them gave up. But persistence is not just the preserve of the famous. Anyone can be persistent. It requires single-mindedness and guts in most cases, a belief that one is right, and an overwhelming personal desire to achieve.

Dame Rennie Fritchie and Stephen Johnson commented:

'My style was to work alongside others rather than to fight generally. There were times when I stood up to be counted, but I never ever felt it necessary to win every battle. I've always been a strategic thinker and I've always had the longer-term goal in mind. What am I trying to achieve overall, rather than how can I notch up one more deal? My strategy has always been to somehow *surround* the goal, rather than to take one shot. The goal has often been blocked but you don't stop and go away, you don't just keep on pushing forward, you just think "All right I'll wait a while and try another approach", and "I'll leave my first position and come back to it later", and "I'll come from this angle or that angle or anywhere that seems possible or flexible".'

Dame Rennie Fritchie

'I think of a man who has been job junting for three years. He has gone out and been regularly "kicked in the guts", but he has kept going time after time, everyday being a new day. And now he's broken out into sunlit uplands. He did that this year, and I am immensely proud of having worked with that man.'

Stephen Johnson

So, number two is *persistence*. Don't give up. If you can't do it one way, look for another. Go round obstacles.

Doing something oneself is relatively easy. You only have to motivate and worry about yourself. Aiming to do something that requires the involvement of other people is quite another matter. You may be in a position of power and can compel people to follow your orders, in which case you have a good start. Keeping them at it may be a bit more difficult, though.

How have charismatic *movers and shakers* motivated others to help achieve their visions and goals in the past? How do they do it now?

Tools of the trade

Movers and shakers achieve through other people. Politicians achieve by influencing their parties, military men their senior officers, religious leaders their disciples, industrialists their senior management teams and sports people their teams. They are all effective leaders as well as being good managers.

We explored the differences between leadership and management at the beginning of this book. My own conclusions are that we have to be able to move along the management/leadership continuum as the need arises. Management requires skills of planning and analysis, whereas leadership requires the ability to synthesize. Synthesis means being able to make two plus two equal five, and that, of course, is what teams are all about. Again, there's nothing new in this! Aesop tells the fable of the single stick versus the bundle. The single sticks are easily broken, whereas a bundle of sticks is practically unbreakable. The bundle has qualities that a single stick does not have – collective strength. Managers and leaders today, probably more than at any other time, need to be good team builders and to understand their role in the team.

Has the manager's role changed? Is it the same as it was 20 years ago? Yes, no, and – it depends. Traditional hierarchical organisations depicted a team as a pyramid with the manager at the top and the team at the bottom – the most important person is the manager. Today, many organisations are beginning to draw their team structures differently, with the team at the top and the manager at the bottom. There are some organisations that go even further and describe their teams as circles, with the manager located outside the circle.

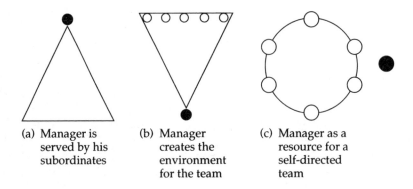

(a) Manager is served by his subordinates

(b) Manager creates the environment for the team

(c) Manager as a resource for a self-directed team

A leader is the person who creates an environment in which all the members of his or her team can give of their best and achieve the team's goals. The manager's role today is to be a coach, facilitator and enabler. The leader's role is to set direction and create an environment in which people *want* to give of their best, working towards stated aims. We have to be able to operate at both ends of the continuum.

It is worth noting that most of the examples of charismatic individuals I have quoted so far are socialised charismatics. Personalised charismatics such as Hitler, Robert Maxwell and Chris Brain, of Nine O'Clock Service notoriety, saw themselves at the top of the pyramid with their followers at the bottom. They certainly had disciples, but their achievements came through the exercise of the personal power they were able to wield. Although status and the situation has much to do with the creation of a charismatic, personal power is vitally important. Roland Howard in *The Rise and Fall of the Nine O'Clock Service* describes the almost unbelievable power of one of today's discredited charismatics:

> 'Brain had the sort of charisma that could elicit massive financial gifts from followers to support his lifestyle; that could persuade young women to form a secretive team of handmaidens who started out by cleaning and shopping but ended up exploring sexual intimacy, convinced that he was ministering to them; that won plaudits from the Archbishop of Canterbury, and internationally known academics, and had senior Anglicans convinced that his radical approach and his church were a future for the Church of England. But, it was also the sort of charisma that made every one freeze when he came in the room.'

Frightening, isn't it? But to return to creating environments in which people are able to give of their best, Peter Sharpe appears to have a real passion for this. He is able to get the best out of his people, and help them get the same out of their people:

> 'I'm one of these naïve people that say the person in front of me is good, that person does not come to work to be bad, does not come to work to fail and wants to improve his or her lot. They have talents, some of which are obvious and some of which are hidden. We should develop them all. My divisional commander at Watford, Paddy Flavin – he is another really charismatic character. Paddy handled the rail crash the other night. I asked him to go to Watford in January of 1995. The division was going down the tubes. I wanted him to go in there and raise it, give it vitality, I want it to be my flagship division. I didn't know how he was going to take it but you would have thought I'd given him a £30,000 a year rise! When he went down to the scene and started running the major incident the other night, he had just about everybody who was on duty doing things. People who were off duty and even people who were on annual leave and heard it on the TV and radio, either turned up at the police station in uniform or phoned in to see if there was anything they could do. That's the measure of the power that man exerted over that division. But it's also saying something to him about those people. People desperately want to do a good job. They want to display all their potential and all their talents.'

Number three is *team leadership*. We all need an understanding of our own role and the skills required to lead a team in the most appropriate way.

> 'Belief in oneself and belief in the others. The best recognition you can have is to create a successful team, not because of belief in yourself, but belief in them.'
>
> *Jean-Marie Descarpentries*

Do as I say, not as I do

Managers in all walks of life seem to attach very little importance to 'example'. People tend to forget that others watch their every move and that every move sends a message to others. Sadly, the most topical examples today are those provided by the 'fat cats' of the corporate world. A 'labourer is worthy of his hire', and I have no problem with individuals earning substantial sums by their own efforts. What is far more difficult to cope with, however, are the examples of individuals walking away with millions as a result of privatisation or golden handshakes on 'retirement' (dismissal?). This tends to happen when individuals at the other end of the scale in the same organisation are being made redundant, taking pay cuts or having minuscule pay rises! The trouble with this kind of example is that it influences people everywhere. No wonder many teachers refer to employees in the manufacturing industry as 'cannon fodder'. Union leaders, journalists and politicians are all influenced by this kind of behaviour and it has done more to damage the reputation of British management than anything else in the last ten years.

Reflecting on his time in the Foreign Office, Sir Antony Acland talked about heading a large organisation. He said that the top person in an institution has to have standards which he or she expects of themselves. They mustn't expect people to do things they are not prepared to do themselves. If they are seen to be slipping off at an early hour, not doing their duty and 'not really sticking to the path, taking the cream, and not biting on the bullet', to mix metaphors, then they would be a successful leader. A leader has to show interest in people, interest in their standards – of living and service terms of service and so on. A leader must do his or her best for his or her people, whilst at the same time not agreeing to every request.

A soldier's view on leadership

'I think that leadership is getting people to do what needs to be done in the best possible way. I think the qualities for doing that are first, example and second, sympathy. Sympathy is the ability above all to understand the needs and interests of those for whom you are responsible down the line, and an ability to communicate in such a way that they will understand, so that they trust you and you can get the best out of them.

Unless senior people are honest over the facts concerning the particular venture in which they are involved and about themselves, I don't think that they can expect people to trust them. Today I think failure is really one of example. This strikes me over and over again when I read that a workforce is going to get an increase of, say, 3 per cent, which may be a few hundred pounds a year, and top management is getting an increase of 9 per cent, which may work out to be double the pay the individual man in the workforce is earning. It seems to be very peculiar that people who are supposed to be intelligent are so insensitive about what their own people must think of them if they behave in this way.'

Sir John Acland

The great machismo

Macho management is all the rage in some organisations. The criteria for 'macho' always includes the amount of time spent at work, as long as it is visible to other people. Here, an individual's value is judged not by what he or she contributes but by the number of hours spent at a desk. Who makes these judgements? Managers. Here we have a managerial example at its very worst. The culprits, normally male, or single female managers may spend up to 16 hours a day at work, or even more. They are first in and last out. That is fine, providing 'first in and last out' spans a reasonable length of time. But 16 out of 24 hours cannot be called reasonable on a daily basis. This is a most destructive example which employees follow because, in the most part, they are terrified of losing their jobs. Of course, there are times when working long hours may be necessary – but not on a consistent basis. (Remember Scrooge? He forced Bob Cratchit to work very long hours.)

Managers are responsible for creating the atmosphere in the working environment. Long hours at work can cause people severe stress and, in the long run, rarely produce the required results or a conducive atmosphere. Today, we have to work smarter, not harder. (Does every activity really add value, or are most of them habit or status preserving?) A manager's role is to create the appropriate environment for the growth and development of every member of the team, not to create excessive and unnecessary stress. A conversation I had with a young manager not long ago went something like this:

'I spend about 14 hours a day at work. At month end, or at the end of the financial year, it can mean working all night.'

'Why do you do it?'

'If I didn't, my manager wouldn't think I was any good. He comes in at 6.30 am every morning and goes about 10 pm. I feel obliged to be here when he is. To be fair, he usually tells me to go about 9 pm.'

'Doesn't he have a home to go to?'

'Yes, but I suppose his wife doesn't mind. He has just had a new baby. I thought things would change a bit but they haven't. Mind you, the MD is no different. He works the same kind of hours and he isn't married so I suppose its understandable for him. But I did think that the new baby would change things.'

'Do you have any hobbies at all?'

'No, not really, I haven't the time. And I often work at the weekend as well so it's a bit difficult.'

I regularly work with senior executive secretaries who work for CEOs, MDs and directors in large organisations all over the world. It does not matter where they come from, a lot of them will work amazing hours. Many of them will be single women and, if they are not, the pressures can be even greater.

Do we live to work or work to live?

If our answer is 'live to work', we have to ensure that people do not feel obliged to follow the example we set for fear of losing their job. What messages do we send to others through our behaviour? Meeting our own personal needs? Problems with relationships at home? Values such that work supersedes family? A mindset which prevents us reviewing our work activities in the light of current applicability and value? A refusal to look at new ways of doing things? A lack of care for the welfare of others? A lack of awareness of the example that we set?

In an earlier chapter I suggested that writing one's own obituary could be a very helpful exercise. Another one involves compiling a list titled 'characteristics of the worst managers I have known'. Having done that, compile another one titled 'characteristics of the best managers I have known.' Then put yourself first in your subordinates', then your peers' and finally your superiors' shoes. Using both lists, which words would they tick as applicable to you? Honesty is important here! If you are very brave, try checking with them. Did you see yourself accurately?

Back to the obituary. How would you want people to remember you? Kind, compassionate, energetic, bloody-minded, aggressive, thoughtful, caring, creative … the list is endless. Having identified what you want to be remembered for, ask yourself 'Is my behaviour congruent with the way I want to be seen? What kind of example am I setting to others?'

Leaders set examples in hundreds of different ways. In his book, *Virgin King*, Tim Jackson describes Richard Branson:

> 'He manages and motivates his staff by example … All day long, he carries around with him a black A4 notebook – standard issue, bought from the Ryman's stationery chain – into which he jots not merely ideas that might be put into use in his businesses, but also names and telephone numbers, notes on conversations, and lists of tasks to carry out … Such is the respect he is held in by his employees that many senior staff in the different Virgin companies now carry the same notebooks with them, and can be seen scribbling down thoughts and notes of conversations in exactly the same way.'

Number four must be – *set a good example.*

> 'It's about how you go about your day-to-day work. For me, a central part of being a role model is about being authentic – genuinely being what you appear to be and being prepared to be vulnerable about your whole self. You have to be your whole self the whole time, practise what you preach, and embody it.'
>
> *Dame Rennie Fritchie*

FAIL TO PLAN, PLAN TO FAIL
(IT IS JUST AS TRUE HERE …)

It is easy to relegate planning and control to the back seat while getting very excited by the passion of leadership and the excitement of motivation. Henry Fayol started off the debate on management with his theory that management is about planning and control and, of course, he is right. *Moving and shaking* is all about making things happen, and effective *moving and shaking* relies on excellent planning and control by someone: not necessarily the leader.

> '… Richard Branson has always been a generator of ideas who needs someone else to follow behind him – attending to the details …'
>
> *Tim Jackson, Virgin King*

> 'The secret of the Kennedy success in politics was not money but meticulous planning and organisation.'
>
> *Rose Fitzgerald Kennedy, Times to Remember*

Many effective and charismatic leaders are brilliant at coming up with the broad strategy, but we need good managers, people with a real talent for planning, organising and controlling, to put their ideas into action. Fergal Quinn, one of Ireland's most charismatic business leaders, is a big picture ideas man. He runs his very successful chain of supermarkets, Superquinn, with his team of colleagues. The ideas, the image and the motivation all come from Fergal Quinn, but the numbers and the organisation are looked after by the other team members. Fergal Quinn does what he is good at and now leaves others to do what they are good at. He is always at pains to point this out, giving others much of the credit for success.

I still have the little gold boomerang stick pin he gave each one of us when he talked to me and my colleagues from the National Australia Bank Group about his boomerang philosophy. What do boomerangs do? They come back. So what must each person do to get customers to come back? Simple and very effective. All his staff wear little gold boomerangs.

Playing to strengths

Anita Roddick does what she is good at – ideas, concepts, image – while others run the Body Shop on a day-to-day basis. The late Laura Ashley was the same. She came up with the designs and was the original inspiration for the business but I remember her telling me that her business was a partnership in which her husband Bernard provided the business brains. Gordon Wills is the ideas man behind the very successful MCB University Press, one of the largest publishers of serialised management journals in the world. His colleague, Dr Keith Howard, and a team of very able individuals run the business.

All of these people have a good grasp of the skills required for planning and control. They do not just abdicate responsibility to others. The vital importance of the managerial versus leadership role is clearly understood, but the people involved play to their strengths. Many household name leaders like Sir John Harvey Jones served their 'apprenticeship' in roles which were primarily management in nature but when they found themselves in a real leadership role, they blossomed. They can really spread their wings unconstrained by what they see as the nitty-gritty detail. Of course, many leaders are excellent planners and combine the two different skills of analysis and synthesis very well. Great military leaders combine these skills. Napoleon, Alexander the Great, Genghis Khan, Montgomery, Nelson and the Duke of Wellington were all pretty good at doing both. Real grasp of detail may mean the difference between life and death.

The point to be made is that we all need to be able to plan because it has a vital role in helping us to achieve our goals. And yet that planning must be flexible and continually responsive to the conditions around us. Rigid plans set in stone are likely to bring an enterprise to its knees very quickly.

The great charismatics understand; and if they do not have these skills, they work together with people who do.

Moving and shaking, making things happen, requires considerable inter-personal skills. Even those individuals who appear to make things happen only for themselves, like Benedict Allen, need good people skills because nothing is achieved without the involvement and cooperation of other people. Benedict is the first to say that he depends on others for his success and, more importantly, his life on many occasions.

YES, YES – BUT WHAT IS THE *REAL* SECRET OF MOVING AND SHAKING?

Quite simply, *energy* – which stems from being in love with yourself and what you do (I hear a big groan at the mention of more psychobabble! I make no apologies – I listened time and time again to my charismatic interviewees describing exactly those feelings) and, if you believe in an ultimate Being, then love of that Being. It is only when we get out of bed in the morning with enthusiasm for the day that we display the real energy which will help us make things happen.

It is very difficult to make things happen when we are not committed to what we are doing. Many, many of us are in jobs that we do not like, feeling trapped by circumstances, mortgages and responsibilities. But it does not have to be like that. Of course, we make commitments which we should honour and have responsibilities we must shoulder but these do *not* go on forever. Anyway, with a little courage and creativity, it is often possible to do things in a different way. The problem is that we get trapped, set in our ways and conditioned to believe that things always have to be so. They do not. We can change things if we want to. We can work at what we want to; we just have to find a way of doing this. It may not happen overnight, but with persistence we can make it happen for ourselves. Sometimes we need a little help and support from friends, family or professional counsellors. We in our turn can provide the same support for others. When we are truly committed to ourselves and what we do, then making things happen comes easily. The formula is very simple – goals, persistence and energy.

SUMMARY

We all have the *potential* to make things happen, but we do not all find the *energy* to make things happen. What do *movers and shakers* do to make things happen? They know what they want to do, and go for it with enthusiasm:

- They are persistent
- They are good team leaders
- They set a good example.

Movers and shakers

- Are passionate about their work
- Have dreams and visions
- Do what they love doing
- Are persistent and totally committed
- Delegate
- Work through people in teams
- Are both able to lead and manage
- Have a good grasp of planning and control skills
- Set excellent examples.

Action points

- Work at what you want to
- Verbalise, and share your dream and vision
- Develop and sustain focus
- Sharpen your team skills
- Develop the ability to move along the leadership–management continuum with ease
- Develop planning and control skills
- Always set excellent examples.

DO YOU PUT YOUR HEAD ABOVE THE PARAPET? ARE YOU ALWAYS VISIBLE?

1. I am known as someone with strong views. This
    - (a) describes me well ☐
    - (b) does not describe me at all ☐
    - (c) is sometimes true ☐

2. Which describes you best?
    - (a) I will always stand up and be counted ☐
    - (b) I prefer a quiet life even when I feel quite strongly about something ☐
    - (c) I prefer not to get involved in contentious matters ☐

3. Colleagues frequently put me forward, nominate me and volunteer me for things
    - (a) true ☐
    - (b) not true ☐
    - (c) sometimes ☐

4. I promote myself
    - (a) all the time ☐
    - (b) sometimes ☐
    - (c) never ☐

5. I would describe myself as thick-skinned
    - (a) yes ☐
    - (b) no, I would not ☐

6. I get very nervous when I am in the limelight
    - (a) yes, I hate it ☐
    - (b) no, I am very happy there ☐
    - (c) a bit of both ☐

7. People who seek publicity must expect everything they get
    - (a) I agree ☐
    - (b) I disagree ☐

8. I am always polite, courteous and respectful towards reception and security staff, secretaries and cleaners
    - (a) always ☐
    - (b) sometimes ☐
    - (c) I do not notice them ☐
    - (d) the question has nothing to do with visibility ☐

9. I work hard and believe that I am well disciplined
   (a) I agree ☐
   (b) I disagree ☐
   (c) sometimes ☐

10. I work at building self-confidence
    (a) all the time ☐
    (b) sometimes ☐
    (c) I do not believe that self-confidence can
       be built ☐

11. I prefer not to stand out from the crowd
    (a) true ☐
    (b) untrue – I am very happy to be different ☐

Score

1. (a) 5	2. (a) 10	3. (a) 5	4. (a) 5	5. (a) 5	6. (a) 5
(b) 1	(b) 0	(b) 0	(b) 3	(b) 0	(b) 0
(c) 2	(c) –1	(c) 2	(c) 0		(c) 3

7. (a) 5	8. (a) 5	9. (a) 5	10. (a) 5	11. (a) 0
(b) 3	(b) 2	(b) 0	(b) 3	(b) 5
	(c) 0	(c) 3	(c) 0	
	(d) –5			

Score ☐

Total available: 60 marks. If you scored:

- Over 55 You manage your visibility very well.
- Between 40 and 55 You are well aware of the price of visibility and are working hard to manage it.
- Between 30 and 40 This is not a comfortable area for you. You need to explore this issue in more depth.
- Under 30 You are very unhappy with personal visibility and consequently may need to avoid it.

Key 6 THE VISIBLE KEY

I did not interview any retiring wallflowers or shrinking violets. Some were modest, some *certainly* were not! Some were well known, others were not! All the charismatic people I interviewed would stand out in any crowd and would definitely make their presence felt. Some would do this quietly, and some with more flamboyance. They were all very *visible*. Have they achieved this by accident or design?

Charismatics *are* visible, almost by definition – and for a number of reasons. They are people who will always stand up and be counted: 'putting one's head over the parapet' makes one very visible. That is one major reason for visibility. Another is that followers raise their charismatic leader's profile and make them visible. They don't keep the person and his or her beliefs a secret. The third reason revolves around the fact that charismatic personalities are happy to be different. They do not mind behaving differently or looking different. They have lots of self-confidence and courage. So they stick out anyway, even if they do nothing out of the ordinary. And, fourthly, some of them seek visibility! And why not? If you've got it, flaunt it.

LEANING OVER THE PARAPET

Sir Winston Churchill was no stranger to fame. He came to public notice very early on in his career:

'Throughout his political career Churchill was ever an outstanding figure, with a magnetic attraction for the limelight. Failures could never abash, nor setbacks dishearten him. Whether his contemporaries were with him or against him, they could never thrust him aside or leave him out of account. And they were often against him, for during a large part of his public life Churchill inspired more interest than confidence. His very cleverness, allied as it was with an element of dare-devilry and schoolboy recklessness, counted against him … Dash and daring are equally unwelcome, for they may land the nation all unawares in some rash adventure or entanglement.'

Malcolm Thompson, Churchill: His Life and Times

It takes a good deal of courage to say what one thinks and not compromise personal values and principles. It can be very uncomfortable and very stressful and can lead to much criticism from one's peers, superiors and subordinates. It is about standing out from the crowd. Charismatic individuals have well-developed personal confidence, together with belief systems that are strong enough to sustain them in the hard times. Peter Sharpe is certainly prepared to say what he thinks, even when it might not suit those in high places:

> 'I'm prepared to put my head above the parapet, which I did the other day with the CS sprays. I don't think the government have got it right. I don't think they have allowed us to trial all of the products which we should have trialed and I think there are some flaws in the way that we trial them, I think we have to be courageous and say so. I want to keep the item at the top of the agenda and that's the way to do it.'

Edwina Currie comes from the same mould and always stands out from the crowd:

> 'I know that I am visible and that I am heard. I am visible because I am a woman in a world substantially dominated by men and because I choose to be, because I wear bright colours which is partly a reaction to not wishing to be seen as a man in dark colours. I'm heard because I like to use words in a very clear way. I can understand complex issues because of my own education and training and I like to translate them into simple clear ideas and language. So those two elements make me stand out a bit from the crowd.'

As a consultant I have the privilege of working within organisations in some depth. Sadly, I often come across organisational cultures which are so strong that they prevent individuals saying what they think or know to be true. Recently I was working within a large global oil company on a series of management development programmes. The first one we ran was difficult and uncomfortable both for faculty and participants because it was about learning new things, changing attitudes and behaviours. However, the independent evaluation carried out at the end of the programme was very positive. All the participants had been interviewed individually and their comments recorded. Our client was delighted and so were we. The second programme was also uncomfortable – so uncomfortable for the participants that they complained to their management. The result was that we were sacked and the results of the first programme discredited and denied. The client did not have the guts to tell the participants to stick with it and his boss didn't have the courage to insist. They all took the view that they must stick together, despite their own views. None of them would stand up and be counted. The macho male culture was just too strong for them. No true charismatic individuals in that organisation!

That does not mean to say that charismatic individuals are not affected by what people say. Most of them are to some degree – but they are not destroyed or deflected by other people's criticism. They will consider what is said, react, and build on the views if they think it appropriate. This, of course, is one of the great dangers with personalised charismatics. Their views are not influenced by others. They do not even listen to anyone else. Hitler did not appear to be influenced by anyone towards the end of his life – neither, I suspect was Robert Maxwell.

Many of the religious and spiritual charismatics were personalised charismatics, such as Rasputin and Georgei Gurdjieff, who held views which, although they might have been developed from the ideas of others, were views that the individual believed were his and his alone. They refused to be challenged on them. This is also true of contemporary religious figures such as Chris Brain, Jim Jones and David Koresh. Socialised charismatics, on the other hand, are dependent upon their followers and others to help them refine and develop their vision.

STRONG VIEWS

People who express strong views are marked out. They become very *visible*. It is as if they cannot be ignored, rather like a ringing telephone. Something has to be done to stop the noise. Society 'deals' with them in a number of different ways. Sometimes they are given 'crank' status. Screaming Lord Sutch of the Monster Raving Loony Party is a good example. Such people are tolerated and indulged, but sidelined. Their views are ignored. Screaming Lord Sutch was sadly missed at the last election, but it is doubtful if many people really knew what he stood for. Some are the subject of intense derision. Although Mary Whitehouse has many followers who share her views, she has been the butt of many a joke and is consistently derided in the media.

On the other hand, a large number of people listened to Sir James Goldsmith of the Referendum Party and he achieved a great deal of credibility despite his party's poor showing in the polls in 1997. Of course, there are many more variables at work in all three examples, but I want to make the point that society's response to people with strong views varies. Strong views are certainly not ignored – the response depends on the prevailing environment within society as a whole.

'Let others lift you above the mass, on their own initiative.'
Stephanie Barrat-Godefroy

White smoke or black smoke? The stove used to burn the ballot papers was less than reliable and puffed grey smoke instead. At the conclave held after the death of Pope Pius XII in 1958, the crowds in St Peter's Square couldn't tell whether the smoke from the Sistine Chapel was white or black. They couldn't tell if the cardinals had elected a new Pope or not.

This ritual burning of the ballot papers describes the progress of what is probably the most famous election process in the world, where a man is lifted above his peers by his peers. It would be unrealistic to think that some electioneering does not go on when the reign of a pontiff appears to be drawing to a close, but I suspect the majority of Catholics would like to think that God has a big say in who is elevated to Peter's Chair. We live in a sceptical world and it is difficult to think of examples in which individuals are chosen to occupy public office or position without putting themselves forward in some way. If elected, a cardinal can refuse the burden of the pontificate, whereas most of the rest of us have to decide before the election and accept nomination.

In theory any male Catholic can be elected Pope. But it is not likely to happen, so it isn't really a career opportunity for anyone outside the Catholic priesthood! However, we can all be headhunted.

'I started to play rugby and it was the first sport I really excelled in. I won my colours and suddenly everybody needs you, you are lifted up a little bit, and then success breeds success and I become a prefect. It's a bit like a swan really.'

Paul Lever

'Visibility means being present with those for whom you are responsible; being seen to understand their problems and taking part where necessary with them in the same difficulties, and sharing the problems that they're facing, whether it be low pay or very uncomfortable living conditions.'

Sir John Acland

BLOWING YOUR OWN TRUMPET

Richard Branson would probably get most people's vote for the best self-publicist around in business today.

> 'Achieving good press has been as important in Branson's business career as making sure that the books balance at the end of the year. From his first days as a magazine publisher and record retailer, Branson knew that descriptions of his ventures as successful and expansionary could become self-fulfilling … It took two factors, however, to turn Branson from a moderately-known eccentric pop millionaire into a fully-fledged celebrity. One was the launch of Virgin Atlantic which gave him the opportunity to indulge his taste for dressing up in a series of outlandish outfits.[1] (The apparent thirst for personal publicity which he then acquired had a great deal to do with the need to compete with British Airways on a shoestring advertising budget.) The other factor in his current fame was the danger involved in his record-breaking sea and balloon crossings of the Atlantic and Pacific. In public, Branson would talk about his thirst for adventure and his love of competition and the outdoors. In Virgin board meetings, he defended the spending of company money on these exercises by saying that they were the cheapest possible way of advertising group companies. By the end of the 1980s, Branson's image as popular hero had become a bankable asset for his businesses, arguably even more valuable than the Virgin brand name itself.'
>
> *Tim Jackson, Virgin King*

I doubt if Branson would indulge in wooing the media if he did not personally enjoy its attentions. Six of one and half-a-dozen of the other, I suspect! And why not, indeed?

Nancy Wise, always one to see things as they are, made the following observation:

> 'I suppose Mother Theresa is one of the great charismatic ladies. She's the one they all say has great charismatic quality. She's a great networker, milks everybody and makes sure she's visible. A bit like Sister Wendy she's a charismatic lady for sure. She's eccentric because she's wearing a totally out-of-date habit that no nun in the world wears! She does it because it makes her very visible.'

---

[1] Biggles-style goggles among other things!

Lord Wakeham, chairman of the Press Complaints Commission, warns that the glare of the media can be very punishing. Branson himself is known to find criticism difficult to cope with, unlike Winston Churchill whose belief in himself was so strong that he always believed the criticism to be misguided. Two of the people I interviewed had very little time for Branson and his image and were adamant that, for them, he was definitely not charismatic. One said:

> 'I don't think Richard is charismatic and don't you kid yourself that he is interested in the welfare of others. Richard is clearly interested in the progression of Richard! I have seen him time and time again when a meeting has been set up with what he calls the "common little people" and he just doesn't turn up! This is just rude! I don't think Richard is charismatic.'

Paul Lever had quite strong feelings about personal visibility:

> 'I think you *have* to be visible as part of the job of leading. However I have real problems with the razzmatazz, "make me famous", people. I despise them, I have no time for them.'

PRIVILEGE AND RESPONSIBILITY

Sir John Harvey Jones said that he was surprised when the producer of the *Troubleshooter* programmes suggested to him that he would not be able to go unnoticed in the future. Everyone would know his face and he would lose his anonymity. And, of course, this turned out to be true. Sir John cannot walk down the street without someone recognising him: neither can Edwina Currie or Barry John. Do they mind? I got the impression that on the whole they don't. However, it means that they have to be polite and courteous all the time which must, on occasion, be very demanding. Sir John's view is that fame brings responsibility with it – responsibility to respond with courtesy and appreciation – and this, more often than not, involves the whole family of the person concerned. Lady Harvey Jones is very conscious of this responsibility and, according to Sir John, plays a large part in helping him meet his self-imposed obligations.

> 'Visibility? The guy who runs the Total Quality for the force says to me, "Your visibility is probably the most important aspect in TQ in the force, it's the profile that you set, the marketing of yourself and the force that matters".'
>
> *Peter Sharpe*

> 'First *do* something, then *be* someone.'
> *Lord Kings Norton*

Good advice for those of us who want to *be* someone!

Charismatic individuals are always known for something else as well as their charisma. It's back again to the idea that charisma does not exist in a vacuum. They might be known for their leadership abilities, skills, personal achievements, views and beliefs, or position and status. The charisma is superimposed on to the person's power base.

In the same way that the environment must be appropriate for the emergence of charismatic individuals, so they must have something to offer. Martin Luther King had his passion for civil rights; Sir John Acland, Peter Sharpe and the Duke of Wellington, their outstanding leadership abilities; Jean-Marie Descarpentries and Heather Rabbatts have a truly uncommon commitment to people; Evelyn Glennie has her incredible musical gift; Barry John his brilliant rugby skills, Tony Buzan his expert knowledge of the brain and Mind Mapping® work; Mo Acland her commitment to nursing; Grethe Hooper Hanson to accelerated learning; and so the list goes on. They all have something to be charismatic about.

Each one of us needs to have something to offer. What is it that we want to offer other people? As suggested in the *vision* chapter, you might like to contemplate writing your obituary to clarify your thoughts here. What do you *want* to be remembered for? What do you think you *will* be remembered for? Ask a good friend for their views on the latter if you dare.

Almost all the well-known people I interviewed became well known as a result of a particular skill, ability or belief. How do they become well known? First of all, they are all very good at what they do. They have worked hard to develop the qualities, skills and abilities that they have. Then, some of them, like Benedict Allen, employ the services of a PR agency to manage their image and to increase their visibility. Or, if they are politicians, they have the local party to promote them once they have been selected. Others use a specialist agency to promote themselves as speakers. They spend a good deal of their time on speaking engagements. Some of them are well-known authors in their own fields. For example, Benedict Allen is a very successful author of travel and exploration books; Dr Aubrey Wilson, Robert Heller, Sir John Harvey Jones and Tony Buzan are management gurus; and Edwina Currie is a successful 'best-seller' author. All of these people regularly speak to large audiences and are good speakers. Are their books a platform or are they good speakers who then write good books? A bit of both, I suspect.

'I also think that I have some appeal to children. I do seem to be recognised by children – I have no idea why. They want me to be their granny, usually! I think it may be because I agree to go on the breakfast programmes that are seen by 2 million children at any one moment. They have a huge audience of about 10 million a week. Many of my colleagues stand on their dignity and will not do this but I think they are crazy – if you have a message, if you have something to say, you should use whatever means are available. You shouldn't pick and choose too much.'

Edwina Currie

Fred Dibnah is no stranger to our television screens, and yet he is not a self-publicist. He is very self-effacing and does not seek or, I suspect, need the limelight. His wife Sue recognises what he does for people:

'Three weeks ago on the South Downs we had 30 people queuing up to meet Fred in torrential rain. Somebody said that they had queued up for a jockey's autograph which turned out to be an illegible scribble. The jockey didn't speak to them either. Whereas Fred behaves just like he has with you today; he stands telling stories. People are quite prepared to queue for two hours because they know when they get to him, he's going to have time for them. And he'll kiss granny and hold the baby and stroke the dog and shake people's hands. Fred says that whenever we feel irritated by this it's important to remember that these people made him what he is today. Sometimes that's what big stars forget.'

I remember going to a school speech day with John Garnett of Industrial Society fame, where he had been asked to give out the prizes. Normally, speakers shake hands with award-winners and leave it at that – but not John Garnett. He had a personal word with every girl who came up to receive her certificate, cup or prize from him! The ceremony took much longer than it should have done and the school staff, not knowing that he would do this, were hopping up and down with anxiety and irritation! I was rather surprised too, but on reflection I thought he was right and still do. I'm sure that the parents didn't mind sitting for a bit longer.

Who's for sago grubs?

Benedict Allen is quite extraordinary. Among many other superb qualities and skills, he has developed the ability to leave his own world behind and step, quite literally, into very primitive worlds. He has his own time machine – in which he can go back to the Stone Age. Unlike most other explorers, he lives with the people he visits just as they live, without any of the trappings of the twentieth century. He hunts as they do, eats what they eat, uses the herb medicines they use and shares their lives. He has a wonderful story (not for the squeamish) in which he describes how he was offered a local delicacy which he knew he must not refuse: two plump wiggling creamy sago grubs, about two inches in length. Bravely, he swallowed them, only to feel them crawling back up his throat! But he won in the end. It does not matter what we choose to be good at, we have to work at it. And it isn't always easy. Sometimes it's like swallowing sago grubs. It requires enormous self-discipline, concentration and determination.

The people I interviewed are not just famous for their charismatic personalities! They are all achievers in their own right. There are rugby players who are as good as Barry John but, lacking his charisma, have not achieved in the same way that he has. One of the most important lessons to be learnt from charismatic people is that they work *very hard* at becoming *very good* at their particular specialisms *and* at their charismatic gifts. Jean-Marie Descarpentries does not like the concept of charisma. He says that he does not believe in it. He is a very effective, but unorthodox strategist and a compelling leader. However, he talks passionately about the need to work hard to develop excellent communication skills. He maintains that the skills of leadership can be learnt but it requires hard work and dedication. He is a very visible man in France and became so in the UK when he was CEO of CarnaudMetalBox.

Charismatics normally get sacked

Unfortunately for Jean-Marie Descarpentries, the British press were none too keen on this very charismatic Frenchman! The Brits, as John Adair of Action Centred Leadership says, are not usually susceptible to charisma. In addition, the results of some American research suggested that the better educated are less likely to regard anyone as charismatic. All this, together with the fact that Descarpentries is not English but French, probably accounted for his lack of popularity in the British press. Charisma can work against one just as much as it can be an asset. More often than not, visible charismatics are sacked somewhere along the line: Churchill and De Gaulle were both sacked by their countries! Edwina Currie and Lady Thatcher did not escape either. And Descarpentries was sacked from

CarnaudMetalBox. He is in good company. The message for the rest of us may lie in the old saying, 'If you can't stand the heat, get out of the kitchen'. Life for very visible people with strong views can be very hot and very uncomfortable.

Hands up who wants to be a dartboard

Charisma and invisibility cannot coexist. Charismatic people cannot be invisible. Neither do they want to hide. They are proud of what they believe in and what they do. They are prepared to take the consequences of their strong views and they are very skilled in expressing these views in a way which attracts followers. The message for the rest of us is very clear. Unless we are happy to stand up and be counted, to put our heads above the parapet in support of our views and what we believe in, we are never likely to be charismatic. And that is a hard one.

Note

The results of my survey appear to contradict both John Adair and the American research. Respondents were all well-educated and identified a great many people as charismatic. However, the response rate from journalists was much lower than for other sectors. Perhaps it is journalists who are the real sceptics?

SUMMARY

- Charismatic individuals are all very visible
- Their strong views make them stand out
- They have the courage to speak the truth as they see it and the self-confidence to be different
- Followers make charismatic leaders visible. They seek visibility for them
- Personal promotion is perfectly acceptable but carries the risk of public criticism
- Being in the public eye can be uncomfortable as well as enjoyable and rewarding
- Fame brings both responsibility and loss of privacy
- Charismatic people are known for their achievements, not just their charisma
- They work hard at their chosen field with discipline, concentration and determination.

Action points

- Stand up and be counted
- Express your views assertively
- Build self-confidence
- Seek visibility and manage the consequences
- Always treat others with respect, courtesy and care.

HOW MYSTERIOUS AND ENIGMATIC ARE YOU?

1. People describe me as exciting to work with
   - (a) true ☐
   - (b) no one has ever described me as exciting ☐

2. Which describes you most accurately?
   - (a) People know everything about me ☐
   - (b) People know very little about me ☐
   - (c) People know most things about me ☐

3. I do not want people to know a lot about me
   - (a) true ☐
   - (b) not true ☐
   - (c) it depends on who it is ☐

4. I talk about myself a lot
   - (a) true ☐
   - (b) I tell people the bare minimum ☐

5. People find me intriguing and ask me questions about very ordinary things about myself
   - (a) often ☐
   - (b) rarely ☐
   - (c) don't know what is meant by the question ☐

6. My charisma comes from
   - (a) my status and position ☐
   - (b) the power I have ☐
   - (c) my achievements ☐
   - (d) my personality ☐

7. I want to know everything about people I admire
   - (a) yes ☐
   - (b) no, I prefer to wonder about them ☐

8. We have a right to know everything about people in public life
   - (a) yes ☐
   - (b) no ☐

9. I find it easy to maintain a distance between myself and subordinates, while at the same time enjoying a good relationship with them
   - (a) true ☐
   - (b) no, it is difficult at times ☐

10. People tease me because I sometimes tell long boring stories!
    (a) true ☐
    (b) untrue ☐

11. At a party I am always surrounded by interested people
    (a) always ☐
    (b) sometimes ☐
    (c) I do not go to parties ☐

Score

1. (a) 5	2. (a) 0	3. (a) 3	4. (a) 0	5. (a) 5	6. (a) 3
(b) 0	(b) 10	(b) 0	(b) 5	(b) 1	(b) 3
	(c) 2	(c) 5		(c) 0	(c) 3
					(d) 5

7. (a) 2	8. (a) 0	9. (a) 5	10. (a) –5	11. (a) 5
(b) 5	(b) 5	(b) 2	(b) 5	(b) 2
				(c) 5

Score ☐

Total available: 60 marks. If you scored:

- Over 55   You are *very* enigmatic and mysterious.
- Between 40 and 55   You are well on your way.
- Between 30 and 40   Self-control will help you if you really want to achieve mystery and enigma.
- Under 30   You are not suited to being mysterious and enigmatic. It may be quite a strain to maintain a distance between yourself and others.

Key 7 THE MYSTERIOUS AND ENIGMATIC KEY

I have started a new club. It is called 'The Most Boring People in the World Club'. Membership is by election (by me, and whoever is unfortunate enough to be around to listen to my rantings after particularly long sessions). At the moment there are four members and I am keen to keep the membership small, for obvious reasons. How do people become eligible for membership? Quite simple really. They must fail to engage my interest and attention even when I am exhausting myself with the effort of trying to be interested. Are the members thought to be worthy of membership by others? Yes and no. People with a higher tolerance level for outwardly uninteresting people might not elect them, but many others would. The criteria that must be attained are quite stringent.

A typically successful member of The Most Boring People in the World Club:

- Speaks in a monotone
- Displays no interest whatsoever in the person they are talking to
- Is oblivious to any verbal or physical feedback during conversations
- Talks about themselves or their views to the exclusion of all else
- Talks about things that are patently of no interest to others
- Tells their listener every little detail about themselves
- Ensures that they are not interrupted
- Returns to talk about their own views if by chance the other person gets a word in
- Displays little energy, other than for hogging the conversation
- Repeats stories monotonously
- Fails to recognise any hints that the conversation should be terminated.

There are three associate members of my MBPW Club. These folk are not fully-fledged world-class bores yet, but with a little more effort they will get there. All the members and associate members, and many others like them, are the opposite of charismatic. They are boring! Do they have to be boring? No: like the rest of us they have innate charisma, but they have not learned to use or develop this potential personal power.

Paul Bailey writing in *The Independent* in April 1993 reminds us that all kinds of things can be boring – not just people:

'About 25 years ago, on a warm afternoon in June, I found myself aching with boredom as I watched a match on the Centre Court at Wimbledon. A tall young American, who looked like Superman, was slogging the ball at his ineffectual opponent, serving ace after ace. Clark Graebner was the name of the slogger-cum-server, and I shall never forget the peculiar ennui he made me endure that afternoon ... he wanted solely to win, and if the spectators were rendered soporific in the process, that wasn't his concern. I think he should have more sympathy for the yawning ranks in the stands by coming to the net just once, perhaps; by experimenting a little. But no, he wasn't even capable of those trifling considerations in his rigid denial of the possibilities of this intrinsically fascinating sport.'

Obviously, membership could rise.

None of the charismatic people I interviewed have any chance of membership of the MBPW Club. All of them are energetic, and for me, *intriguing*. I wanted to know more about them. I found them, almost without exception, *exciting, enigmatic and mysterious*. However, some of them felt that they were not enigmatic at all, and they had no wish to be so. Sue Dibnah says of Fred:

'Yes, lots of people say that they have never written to anybody. I think because Fred has no airs and graces about him ... that's what attracts most people, he is like the guy next door, their dad, their grandad, their uncle, somebody who lives down the road from them. They feel they can write to him and they'll not be laughed at, even though he's got a sort of a star status.'

For others, it was important to retain a significant amount of distance and secrecy, particularly if they found themselves in the public eye. They had a strong need for preservation and secrecy. A private life is a private life and, although they were prepared to talk about more personal aspects of themselves, they maintained a private inner area which was very important to them.

Evelyn Glennie and Benedict Allen put it this way:

'Just thinking about the people who write in – they feel that I am quite outgoing, that I am accessible, and they can talk to me. And then there must be the other aspect where there is a kind of unknown side, a mysterious side ... this is true of anyone who is well known. You're totally accessible once you are on stage. But there just has to be a kind of distance as well. This is one of the problems of the Internet. In one respect it's helpful, but in another it isn't because anyone can call you up or enter your home and you feel obliged to answer them. It's given accessibility a new meaning! I'm trying to work out how much I want to be involved because what can happen is quite overwhelming. It has real advantages in that people can say "I would like to come to your concert", or "When are you playing in our area?" and you can give them a quick answer but there is the other side. They may invade your privacy because it's so easy to do.'

Evelyn Glennie

'Yes, I think I'm incredibly enigmatic. I think I am because people seem to be puzzled about my motivation, what really drives me. I think I'm very misunderstood – it always sounds terribly self-indulgent to say that. When they first hear about me, a lot of people assume I'm the Indiana Jones character. Maybe, often unconsciously, I've played it up in that I know people want to hear about the stories about the time a snake came and almost "got me" and crocodiles and alligators. They want to know about that and it does draw people in immediately. I sometimes wonder about a lot of my explorer contemporaries. They seem to be driven by some sort of insecurity and they've said that they're trying to please their fathers or something. I had this lovely stable family background, I shouldn't have any need except that I was the youngest child – but that happens to a lot of others. Yes, I am an enigma and I think I am very private. That encourages me to put up a final wall of defence that keeps me hidden away down there. I suppose what I'm doing is creating an elaborate persona which confuses people and therefore it stops them getting deep inside me .'

Benedict Allen

THE HOUSE OF WINDSOR

In the UK the charisma of the monarchy depends on mystique, secrecy, separateness and difference. It depends on vertical distance between monarch and subjects. It depends on the people *not* knowing everything about the reigning family. The crisis within the House of Windsor is due in no small part to the media exposure that all members of the Royal Family have had since the showing of the BBC film *Royal Family* in 1969. David Attenborough is quoted as saying that the monarchy would be killed by this film: 'The whole institution depends on the mystique of the tribal chief in his hut. If any member of the tribe ever sees inside his hut, then the whole system of the tribal chieftain is damaged ...'. The charisma of the Royal Family does not belong to individual persons, although a number of them were listed as being charismatic in the survey. The charisma belongs to the institution but it is dependent on the cloak of secrecy and mystery surrounding the incumbent individuals. In the 1950s and 1960s people knew exactly what they wanted from the monarchy – and what they didn't want:

'And nobody wanted the Royal Family to be like film stars, their mood swings, marital rows and favourite restaurants made into the subject of newspaper articles. People revered the Crown, but they were not really interested in the Queen, for the very simple reason that she is not really interesting.'

'Nearly all Royal jokes of the last 40 years ... have been gentle meditations on the Queen's essential dullness ... produced jokes about the essentially bourgeois qualities of the Queen and her family, the fact that they were unfashionably dressed, dowdy and intellectually limited.'

A N Wilson, The Rise and Fall of the House of Windsor

The viewing figures for the 1969 *Royal Family* film were astounding – 23 million in the UK alone. It is doubtful that any such film would achieve such figures today. True, millions tuned in to watch Diana, Princess of Wales, talk about her marriage but we watched that for quite different reasons! The magic is fast disappearing, although the public still turns out to greet members of the Royal Family whenever they appear (I did when the Queen came to Buckingham in 1996).

DID YOU FANTASISE ABOUT YOUR TEACHERS?

The charisma of status, power and position can so easily be destroyed unless the mysterious enigmatic nature of the interaction between role, incumbent and followers is preserved. This does not just apply to the Royal Family. It is true for many of the professions: teachers and doctors, for example. On the whole, children respected and responded to the authority of teachers. The national teacher's strike of 1984 showed children and their parents that teachers were just the same as anyone else. For many the mystique surrounding teachers dissolved in a few weeks and there are some including myself (as an ex-teacher) who would say that the teaching profession has never recovered its position in society. The medical profession, on the other hand, is fighting a rearguard action to try to preserve the secrecy and mystery of medical power and position. They realise that if the mystery is dissolved they will lose a great deal of the status they have enjoyed for over 150 years. People will question their views and decisions far more than they do now, and litigation will become commonplace.

THE IMPORTANCE OF MYSTERY

'True charisma has to have the mystery that means it is not totally recognisable otherwise it could become totally hideous.'

Mo Acland

What can we learn from the demise of institutional charismatic power? The first thing to recognise is the existence and nature of this charisma in the first place. If our charisma depends on the mystery of power, position and status and we wish to keep that charisma, we must protect the mystery. So, no telling all. No being always available and 'on tap'. No saying what you really think if your charisma depends upon your *not* expressing your views. People cannot scrap and argue over what you think if you have not told them! Betty Boothroyd has maintained the institutional charisma of the office of Speaker of the House of Commons and in so doing has further developed her personal charisma. We do not know what she thinks about the junketings of our elected representatives. However, in most cases, in these days of 'one nation' and equality, we might be better advised to develop and maintain our personal charisma rather than rely on institutional charisma which is so vulnerable to public scrutiny and the devastating attentions of the media.

Peter Sharpe thinks he is enigmatic – although maybe he was being a little tongue-in-cheek:

'Enigma, yes. Intriguing, yes – they follow me sometimes out of intrigue. Mysterious, yes. I'm often mysterious, but at least they know now that I've got no hidden agendas. I think that is an enormous waste of energy. Exciting, yes – anybody who's driven with me knows I'm exciting. Captivating, yes – a couple of beers and I'll captivate anybody. Yes, I've got one or two secrets, and I've got some fears too.'

Benedict Allen had some additional thoughts about mystery and enigma, which I think are very applicable everywhere:

'Characters like Pablito, and Willy in the desert, have an aloofness. They have this monarch-like stature. Much of their success was that they deliberately kept a little bit of magic around them. But I think what helped them keep their stature was that they were a little bit separated from the world. To some extent it was the people around them who wanted that; *they* needed to have certain people separated, people like Willy and Pablito.'

A CONTROVERSIAL KEY

Mystery and enigma was the most controversial key as far as my intervie-wees were concerned. They were divided on whether this was a desirable attribute or not. I have included it because I am convinced that mystery and enigma can be very positive attributes. It is one of the keys that sets charismatic individuals apart. They are not the same as everyone else, and for me their charisma depends on my not knowing everything about them. I do not want to know that they have feet of clay. I do not want the media to expose every unimportant little peccadillo about my charismatic heroes and heroines. However, neither do I want them to pretend that they are something that they are not. I *do* want to know if they are fundamentally dishonest. This is a matter of judgement, of course, but I wish that judge-ment were exercised rather than the media's enthusiasm for salaciousness and sales figures. We would all be well advised to heed the proverb 'He that is without sin among you, let him first cast a stone ...'. If we knew everything about everyone we would have no heroes and heroines, and we do need these models. Just imagine how colourless life would be with-out the great charismatics.

Reverse the formula at the beginning of the chapter to make sure that you are not a candidate for the MBPW Club. This will ensure a basic level of mystery and enigma! An individual *lacking* qualification for member-ship:

- Does not speak in a monotone
- Displays interest in the person they are talking to
- Is aware of any verbal or physical feedback during conversations
- Does not talk about themselves or their views to the exclusion of all else
- Does not tell people everything about themselves
- Does not talk about things that are patently of no interest to others
- Welcomes other people into the conversation
- Ensures a balance between themselves and the other person
- Displays energy
- Does not repeat stories monotonously
- Recognises hints that the conversation should be terminated.

REAL MAGIC

The people who have real charisma for each one of us individually are the ones who have real magic. They can transport us into other worlds, they can make us feel really good, and they can inspire us to do things that we would not normally do. They are not wholly attainable. That is important.

Magic is about not knowing how something is done. It is beyond our understanding. It is a mystery.

Can we all be mysterious and enigmatic?

To some extent, if we want to be; some people are like this quite naturally. If and when it is appropriate. If we are comfortable with the idea of keeping a part of ourselves for ourselves alone. Some of us are naturally mysterious and enigmatic. Others are not. An awareness of the contribution that mystery and enigma can make to the way we present ourselves allows us to decide how we wish to be seen. However, the *real* message is – *don't be boring*!

SUMMARY

- Charismatic people are energetic, intriguing, exciting, enigmatic and mysterious
- Status, power and position have their own charisma
- Charisma can be destroyed by familiarity
- Mystery preserves charisma.

Action points

- Identify the source of your charisma
- Listen twice as much as you speak
- Recognise and avoid threats to your mysterious and enigmatic aura
- Ensure that you are not eligible for the MBPW Club.

PART 3

Managing Charisma

WILL YOU BECOME INSUFFERABLE?

4

If you follow the action points at the ends of previous chapters religiously, will you become insufferable?

YES, NO – AND MAYBE!

The antidote to insufferability is humility. So, the question might be better phrased, 'Do you have a good dose of humility?' ('Are you humble?' does not read so well and calls Uriah Heep to mind. Uriah Heep, the creepy character in Charles Dickens' *David Copperfield* was a real enthusiast for humility, being 'much too 'umble'. However, his understanding of humility and his false modesty left a great deal to be desired.)

We can all fall into the trap of arrogance and insufferability unless we tread warily. Exhortations to avoid this disaster litter both religious writing and literature. Remember Christian and Hopeful meeting Vain-Confidence in Bunyan's *Pilgrim's Progress*? Vain-Confidence is on his way to the Celestial Gate. Christian and Hopeful follow him but unfortunately Vain-Confidence, 'not seeing the way before him, fell into a deep pit, which was on purpose there made by the prince of those grounds to catch vain-glorious fools withal, and was dashed to pieces with his fall'. We can't say we haven't been warned. Of course, John Bunyan goes on to provide us with a solution in the Valley of Humiliation, where 'many labouring men have got good estates in this Valley of Humiliation; for God resisteth the proud, but giveth grace to the humble'.

In 1977 I was Deputy Governor of Her Majesty's Borstal Bullwood Hall and one day, out of the blue, I received a telephone call from a Major General Richard Clutterbuck. I had no idea who he was or, indeed, why such an elevated individual should want to talk to me. It transpired that he wanted to meet to talk about young female criminals. I hope that I was able to help him, for he gave me so much. He was the first person in my adult career who made me feel really important. He listened carefully and never interrupted. He always respected my opinion; if he disagreed, we would discuss the issue on an equal basis. He always behaved as if the things I had to say were worth listening to. This was a totally new experience for me as a very small cog in the prison service machine, and one that I have never forgotten. His ability to put his own ego on hold and focus on another individual years younger than himself, and really very insignificant, made me feel like a million dollars! And that is what the real charismatics do. They give their followers a sense of importance and belonging. Richard became a good friend but, even now, he still has the same effect on me. He still makes me feel good about myself. Dr Aubrey Wilson has the same gift. I met Aubrey when I was an inexperienced faculty member at the International Management Centres and he was *the* services marketing guru in the UK (he still is). Both these men have the gift of care and respect for others which transcends their own ego.

> 'If you can talk with crowds and keep your virtue,
> Or walk with Kings – nor lose the common touch …
> Yours is the earth and everything that's in it
> And – which is more- you'll be a Man, my son.'
>
> *Rudyard Kipling*

Some years ago I was introduced to the Prince of Wales. I remember the event very clearly. Although I knew that he would have been very well briefed and that I was only one of many in the line-up, I was amazed that he made a personal comment to me, indicating that he had indeed done his homework. He didn't just reel it off either. He commented as if he meant it. Imagine what effect the chairman's visit would have on employees if all chairmen had the gift of being able to make people feel good. Imagine what would happen if all of us could do this. I don't know if Prince Charles does this naturally or not – but if he doesn't, then he has learnt to do it well.

Diana, Princess of Wales, appeared to be a 'natural' with people in all walks of life. She was extraordinarily popular wherever she went in the world, and this popularity did not seem to diminish after her divorce. Her focus on those with HIV appeared to have had a very beneficial influence on the public's view of the disease. If we are to believe the HIV sufferers themselves, they feel that she was personally interested in them and showed real care and concern for them.

I once had the misfortune to sit next to a Tory grandee at a lunch and he did *not* have the 'common touch', for that is what it is. I have never met such an arrogant individual and, although his speech was good, he left a lasting impression of arrogance, bad manners and rudeness. But perhaps he showed his true colours? If I had influence in any political party I would insist that everyone representing the party spent time examining the effects of their personal behaviour on the party's image. And, of course, that is what Tony Blair appears to have done. There can be no doubt that the Tory Party's collective arrogance contributed to their defeat in the 1997 election. How many of us think about the effect that our behaviour has upon our peers and those we manage or lead?

Nelson Mandela has had a dramatic impact on people all over the world. Heather Rabbbatts met him when he came to the UK in 1996:

'Nelson Mandela came to Brixton. Obviously we all know about his history, and we wondered how he could survive those years. The thing about him is that he truly does not have, or you don't feel it anyway, any sense of bitterness, so in his contact with you or anybody he has almost a sense of divinity. When we were walking together people were saying: "We just want to touch him". I thought that if there was going to be the Second Coming, it would be Nelson Mandela. In the midst of screaming crowds he would talk to the young girl, the old man, everyone. And he would be listening with both ears – he wouldn't be distracted by anything else; he was totally engaged. When he came out of the car after the official meeting, the first person's hand he shook was the security guard at the bottom of the steps who never thought he was part of it at all. Mandela just does it, he doesn't think about it. He was staying at the Dorchester and the guy who works on the door, who I vaguely know, said to me that President Mandela went round in the very early hours of the Saturday morning at about three o'clock, and shook every member of the night staff by the hand. You could see that these people who are never counted, who are the unsung heroes, all the cleaners, the porters, were amazed. They felt cared for. I think he has that absolute serenity which is just awesome.'

All of the charismatics I interviewed, except one, made me feel good. Despite the fact that I was interviewing them rather than having a conversation with them, they made me feel important. They made every attempt to put me at my ease and, as well as answering questions, they were all excellent listeners. Their body language was encouraging and empathetic. They gave me time and many of them had prepared for the interview. The whole experience of meeting so many special people was very motivating. It wasn't just encouragement to write the book. They shared their enthusiasm for life with me.

However, one person didn't make me feel good. I felt as if I was something to be 'fitted in', which of course I was. Although this individual provided me with excellent material, for which I am very grateful, I did not feel that I was in the presence of a charismatic. There was no real interaction between us. There was lots of energy about but it was not directed at me. For me, this person was not charismatic. Arrogance and insufferability came to mind very early on! But this was obviously not true for the people who named the individual concerned.

meg'alo – Gk *megas* great, as: *~mānia*, insanity of self-exaltation, passion for big things; *~saurus*, extinct genus of huge carnivorous lizards.

From the Concise Oxford Dictionary

For some it is not so much insufferability as megalomania and the description of 'huge carnivorous lizard' is often very apt. The name 'Robert Maxwell' comes to mind. I spoke to many people who knew Maxwell personally and, without exception, they all said that he was certainly charismatic – but for some of them the description 'megalomaniac' would be more accurate. So where did he go wrong? Indeed, did he go wrong, or was he always consumed by the insanity of self-exaltation? Aubrey Wilson felt that:

> 'Robert Maxwell had enormous charisma – there is no question about that – but only when he wanted to use it. He has been demonised, and he was a demon, but he had tremendous force – he was one of the most charismatic people I have met.'

Lady Thatcher was consistently identified as charismatic in the survey, but for many she is a very negative figure. Many people say quite openly that they 'hate' her – and hate is a very strong word. For them, megalomaniac is an accurate description of her. Stephen Johnson thought she was charismatic:

> 'If you talk to people who worked closely with her, the effect she had on an entire building simply by being in it was noticeable. I remember talking to a man who was on her staff, and he described it like a "rustling sensation and you knew she was out of Downing Street and into the Cabinet Office. People paled and became very confused". She had vast intellectual power and huge courage. She was a tough woman and could bully. Looking at later performances a hubris developed, overconfidence and a tendency to be imperious and dismissive and all these things. But in the end, like many people she lost sight of her own mortality and became an almost classically tragic figure ... an old sobbing woman leaving Downing Street for the last time.'

It seems to me that as Prime Minister, Lady Thatcher was ill served by the current political system. She should have had a court jester or fool to reflect her behaviour to her. She successfully reduced criticism from within the Cabinet by getting rid of those who did not agree with her politics or her behaviour. True, court jesters and fools sometimes lost their heads – but far less frequently than Lady Thatcher's ministers lost their posts.

> 'On one occasion the "merry villain" was seated at the window of the King's dressing room, reading one of his licentious plays, while Charles was engaged with his toilette. The monarch must have been

under some influence of decency of spirit that morning, for he asked Killigrew (the merry villain) what he would be able to say in the next world in defence of the idle words of his comedies. Tom replied that he would be able to make better defence for his "idle words" than the King could for his idle promises, which were made only to be broken, and which caused more ruin than any of the aforesaid idle words in any of his own comedies.'

Dr John Doran (1858), The History of Court Fools

How many ministers can claim to have been so brave? Perhaps the media has taken over the role of fool, but I think not. The press has its own agenda. The fool's role was different.

Pia Helena Ormerod reflected on the root of Lady Thatcher's charisma:

'I don't think she is charismatic now. I think she needed the power base to be charismatic. Not only did power corrupt but what corrupted her even more than her own power was the fact that people around her allowed themselves to be dominated by her. I also think that she would have been a much better leader if she'd have dared to listen.'

IT'S ALL GREEK TO ME

The Ancient Greeks believed in four cardinal virtues – courage, temperance, justice and wisdom – and these represented the ideal of a balanced and controlled personality. They believed that hubris, or arrogance, destroyed the cardinal virtues. In Greek mythology, Nemesis was an avenging goddess who represented the anger of the gods against all who were proud, insolent and insulting (particularly towards the gods themselves). She was the avenger of arrogant presumption and the punisher of extraordinary crimes. The Greeks recognised that arrogance grows and that it can create other evils as great as itself. Unbridled arrogance shocked them morally, politically and aesthetically. Arrogance was not the same as ambition because ambition required self-control and, frequently, self-sacrifice. Arrogance was regarded as the worst of all evils because it undermined attempts to achieve balance and harmony within the personality and destroyed social obligations. Hitler is a clear illustration that these ideas are as accurate and relevant in the twentieth century as they were for the ancient world. His self-exaltation and arrogance destroyed nations and killed millions on a scale that the Ancient Greeks could not even have imagined.

My interviewees had some interesting things to say about arrogance. I have included a selection of their views, which emphasise the pitfalls to be avoided and the dangers of arrogance.

'If you're not arrogant at the start there's no problem. You can only train something which is already there.'

Barry John

'My wife feels that I am very arrogant. I go through life being me and as far as I am concerned, the chips can fall where they may. I want people to like or dislike me for what I am. I don't want to do things just to make people like me. I am self-indulgent to that extent. I don't set out to be bloody rude to people but, nevertheless, I will not bend to make myself, or appear to bend or project myself into something, merely because that audience or that group of people might prefer. We all of us know professional charmers. You can see the buggers at parties and you can see them switching on. They switch it on for some people and they don't bother with others. I have nothing but contempt for that.'

Sir John Harvey Jones

'I respected a lot of what Mrs Thatcher achieved early on. But nobody ought to be Prime Minister for as long as she was. As commanding officer of a battalion in the army you were absolute god and it would be quite wrong for anyone to do that job for more than two or three years. The real reason is that you get out of touch, you begin to think that you know everything and are so much better informed and so much more experienced that I don't think you listen to other people at all. So she appeared to become more and more arrogant.'

Sir John Acland

'The moment you think that you are a worthy person, you are not charismatic any more. You become arrogant, you lose sensitivity to other people's needs, you become a poorer communicator. Communication is about figuring out what is going to convince the other person. If you are only ever listening to your own point of view you fail to do it. Margaret Thatcher stopped listening in 1989. After ten years of being one of our great prime ministers, when she was renowned for listening hard and picking other people's brains, she changed. After 1989 she believed all the propaganda about how great she was and stopped listening. She then went badly wrong and only lasted another 18 months and she hasn't been listening to anyone since! It's a great tragedy'.

Edwina Currie

'I am not good with individuals except as part of a big scene. Maybe if you are too involved with the individual you can't have the big picture. Everyone tells me I have a gigantic ego – if that means I am appallingly self-confident once I have made my mind up and I am determined, then OK – but I don't think I am egotistical or arrogant.'

Gordon Wills

'I sat next to Maxwell. He was impressive, quite overwhelming in his physical presence because he was a big guy – you really felt over-powered by this great fellow. He was a bully – breathtaking. I was quite young and I didn't have a particularly firm argument or any-thing and I remember sitting there being quite cowed and bullied by this incredible energy. I don't know whether that was charismatic or not. I don't know that he attracted people to him particularly. I wouldn't have thought that he was the sort of guy who would excite you to want to go and work with him.

I would have thought that if you really thought you had charisma it's a "helluva" responsibility, endlessly daunting I think. I know that I can "wow" an audience but I tend not to because it is a big responsi-bility and I'm always slightly bothered about it. I tend to quite delib-erately play it down. I think for me it's a bit dangerous, I very rarely play to my full strength.'

Nancy Wise

My colleague Les Williams worked for Robert Maxwell and knew him very well. He saw both the good and bad sides of Maxwell, but it seems that the bad outweighed the good:

'He had an essential energy. Even when he wasn't well, and he wasn't in good health a lot of the time, never ever once during the time that I knew him did his energy desert him, he was just non-stop. Nothing ever satisfied him.

Sam Wright, our personnel consultant, was absolutely correct. He said that as far as Robert Maxwell was concerned there were two classes of people in the world: one was Robert Maxwell, two was everybody else. And everybody else included family, senior, junior employees – it didn't matter, they were the other class of people; roy-alty – it didn't matter, they were the other class of people. People could go to him with good ideas but they didn't stay with their ideas. He took the idea and he drove them forward. If they were to become part of what was going to go on next, they became his ideas. People stayed with him because he was two people. On a good day, it was like working with your very favourite old uncle. But they happened about one in 12. On a bad day he was a monster. He used to devour people and just tear them up and throw them away. He was awful. The other thing about charisma is fear, and a lot of people were seri-ously frightened of him and with good reason; because he was extra-ordinarily wicked when he was crossed. Terrible. He would just discard people without even thinking. But he had that kind of energy and enthusiasm that really carries you along.'

At the end of the day it's all about responsibility. True socialised charismatics have a very well-developed sense of personal responsibility. They understand the power they have and know that they must use this responsibly and with integrity. The absence of responsibility is more characteristic of personalised charismatics; the dangerous charismatics. Robert Maxwell certainly felt no personal responsibility for those he influenced or involved! Paul Lever, a socialised charismatic, reflected on getting it wrong:

> 'There was tremendous resistance to change, there was no way that those men were going to move. They gave all sorts of excuses and reasons; even the dog wouldn't like it! That tested my ability to communicate any charisma I had. This ability to weld people together is a frightening thing in a way. Because if you get it wrong you take everybody with you.'
>
> *Paul Lever*

OK ... HOW CAN I AVOID ARROGANCE AND INSUFFERABILITY?

The secret is simple. Individuals who are more interested in other people than themselves cannot be insufferable or indeed arrogant. Those who have a personal self-confidence stemming from the centre of the onion are very unlikely to be insufferable or arrogant. It's all about working at oneself on the one hand, and forgetting oneself on the other.

Unfortunately for me, when I was an Assistant Governor at Holloway Prison in the 1970s, the principal officer on duty one weekend radioed through to me asking if I would come to the gate to deal with some difficult visitors. She needed the 'most arrogant person' she could think of and could I come? Arrogance has its uses, I suppose ...

SUMMARY

The antidote to insufferability is humility. Those with the 'common touch' inspire others with a sense of their own importance and personal value.

The Greeks believed that :

- Arrogance destroys the four cardinal virtues – courage, temperance, justice and wisdom
- Ambition requires self-control and self-sacrifice
- Arrogance undermines balance and harmony within personality and destroys social obligations.

Action points

- Constantly review the effect of your personal behaviour on family, colleagues and staff
- Listen! Listen! Listen!
- Continuously develop and maintain a greater interest in other people rather than yourself.

WHAT SHOULD YOUR PERSONAL DEVELOPMENT PLAN CONTAIN?

5

Lots of exciting things that you *want* to do, because if it doesn't you probably won't stick to your plan or complete it.

Charismatic individuals are exciting. They do exciting things and they are exciting to be around. If we want to develop our charismatic attributes, stands to reason that the doing of this ought to be exciting too. This does not mean to say that it won't be hard work, but it shouldn't be a chore. If it is, then it isn't really important. Charisma is about energy and enthusiasm. We need to release the energy and enthusiasm for developing our own charisma from within us. If this is something we really *want* to do, then the energy will bubble up. I found being around all the very special people I interviewed very liberating. They almost gave me permission to feel the way I wanted to, to do the things I wanted to, and behave in the way I wanted to. Because that is what *they* do. Charismatics are their own people, doing 'their own thing'. The majority of other folk do what they think other people want them to do, both at home and at work.

Throughout the book I have tried to create an awareness of the attributes that make people charismatic – the seven Keys to Charisma. Some keys, such as the ability to communicate, are more commonplace than others, but the level of expertise required is out of the ordinary and greater than that most of us experience or practise everyday. Even in the more commonplace, there is much for us to learn.

Planning is normally a left-brain, very systematic, activity, which requires a disciplined approach. This must be coupled with the work of the right brain which encourages synthesis and creativity, particularly when developing and setting personal direction and goals. Creative approaches include a number of useful activities. For example, use a Mind Map® for planning rather than the more conventional forms I have used in this chapter. Make a collection of articles, quotations or pictures which illustrate some of the attributes that you want to develop. Interview the people around you who you consider charismatic; ask them to talk about the characteristics you find most attractive. Pretend that you are writing a novel; draw a pen picture of the kind of charismatic person you would like for the central character. Try out new behaviours. See how they work for you.

Creating a plan which is tangible, which you can be proud of, and which gives you pleasure to look at is most important. Buy a special notebook, create a special file on your PC, or put together a new ring-binder. Do something which makes you feel that your plan is important and significant. Or, if you are one of those people who sees books as tools to be used, write on the endpapers of this book! Whatever – but make it special in your mind. Charismatic people are special, and they do special things.

To recap, what are the areas for personal development, the seven Keys of Charisma?

- Confidence
- Vision
- Communication
- Style
- Visibility
- Moving and shaking
- Mystery and enigma.

What other ideas should we look at?

- The managerial decathlete
- The actor manager
- Personal mission statement
- 360° feedback.

Are there any other ideas and concepts which are particularly attractive to you, or of particular relevance?

Where am I now?
Where do I want to be ?
How do I get there?

What is good for business is very often good for people. These are the three questions which are answered in any good business plan, and they work very well for people too. I propose to use this format as a basis for an individual personal development plan.

WHERE AM I NOW?

Identifying a starting point is important. How else shall we judge progress? How else can we see how far we have come? The first part of a personal development plan must be an audit of your current position.

- Identify a charismatic individual you think really gets it right for each of the Keys of Charisma. Someone who really inspires you. For example, who for you, embodies all the attributes of a brilliant communicator? Who has great style? These should become your role models. Enter an appropriate score for each role model on the charismatic star. If they are good role models they are likely to achieve scores in the 50s–60s

- At the beginning of each chapter there is a questionnaire which, if completed and scored, will help you identify where you are as far as each of the Keys of Charisma are concerned. Plot your scores on the Star diagram below

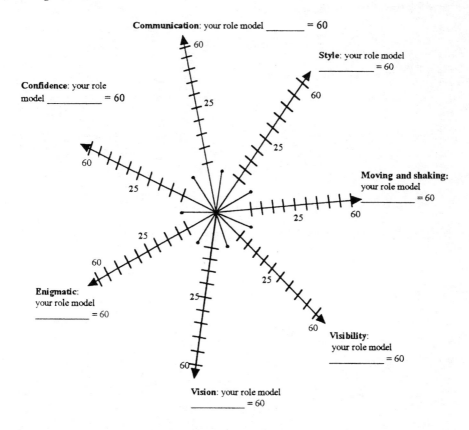

- Look back at the summaries for each of the Keys of Charisma. Are there any particular aspects within each key that you want to identify as areas for development? List these:

  - ....
  - ....
  - ....
  - ....
  - ....

- Do you have an existing written personal mission statement? If not, do you want to write one?
- Summarise your current position using your answers to the questions above. Use the table below if this is helpful.

Charismatic attribute	Score from the charismatic star	Your current position
		(ie where you think you are – be brief, but identify specific aspects)

Key 1 Confidence		
Key 2 Vision		
Key 3 Communication		
Key 4 Style		
Key 5 Visibility		
Key 6 'Moving and shaking'		
Key 7 Mystery and enigma		

Have you written a personal mission statement?	yes/no	comment
Other areas you want to look at	identify	• • • •
Information from 360° feedback (What do other people think about the way you behave?)		their comments

This audit should provide you with a good summary of where you are now in the charismatic stakes. The next thing to do is answer the question: *Where do I want to get to?* Setting direction and goals is always the most difficult bit.

- Look back at the Charismatic Star. With your role models in mind, what do you want to do to improve and enhance your performance in each area?
- Do you want to write a personal mission statement?
- What did you deduce from your 360° feedback? List the areas you need to work on
- Did you identify any other areas for development?

If it's helpful, use the table below to clarify your thoughts.

Charismatic attribute	What would you like to be able to do? What would you like to improve or enhance?
Key 1 Confidence	
Key 2 Vision	
Key 3 Communication	
Key 4 Style	
Key 5 Visibility	
Key 6 'Moving and shaking'	
Key 7 Mystery and enigma	
Personal mission statement	
Other areas	
Aspects identified from 360° feedback	

Now for the $64,000 question:

HOW DO I GET THERE?

The 'how' involves creative thinking, the identification of opportunities, enhancing our 'awareness', and determination and courage. It takes courage to be different and to change behaviours and attitudes that we have become all too familiar with over the years. It often involves major changes in observable behaviour which will probably surprise others, and even shock them.

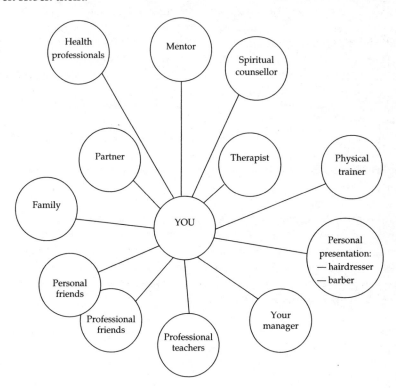

Your personal team

Personal development can be very lonely. Decathletes have coaches and support teams and there is no reason why we cannot put together our own team. Most of us will already have one, but may not have looked at our friends and colleagues in this way before. Think of all the people who keep you in good working order and 'on the road'. Your partner, family, friends, doctor, hairdresser, dentist, counsellor, work colleagues, therapist or manager, for example. Each one of these people contributes towards your well-being in some way or another. In turn, we are members of other people's support teams. This is not just a one-way activity. It goes without saying that the more enthusiastic a member you are of other people's support teams, the more help and support you will enjoy from your own team.

Not everyone likes sharing personal confidences and it may be that you would prefer to work on your plan alone. There is nothing wrong in this at all. However, socialised charismatics tend to have very strong relationships with a whole range of people and actively seek and enjoy support and help from others.

Some of the suggestions I have made in the book may appear at first sight to be rather way out: for example, 'managers are actors and should go to acting school'. This is a serious suggestion and one that can only help towards enhanced presentation skills. However, if you feel that you can't face this one, enrol on a good presentation skills course. But remember that the acting class will be different. You will meet different people and do very different things! And it will probably be more challenging and more interesting – and more exciting. Join an amateur dramatic society – why not?

You may want to identify areas in which you can be more courageous than normal, to find opportunities to 'stand up and be counted'. You might want to rethink your wardrobe and dress the way *you* want to, rather than how you think you ought to. You might decide that you need some help and support to sort yourself out. Be really 'gutsy' and find a counsellor or therapist to support you as you do this. If you feel really brave and haven't already done this, look for 360° feedback: this means asking all kinds of people for feedback on your behaviour in different situations. Friends, family, work colleagues – anyone who is in a position to give you good honest constructive help. Again, if it is helpful use the form below to help you draw up your plan.

Key	What do I want to achieve?	How can I do this? Who can help?	By when? (date)	Date done	Comments
Key 1 Confidence					
Key 2 Vision					
Key 3 Communication					
Key 4 Style					
Key 5 Visibility					
Key 6 Moving and shaking					
Key 7 Mystery and enigma					

Personal mission statement	
Other areas	

TAKE 1 ... ACTION!

Having drawn up your plan, the next task is to put it into action. This may take some time, and it may not be easy. Why not add a mentor to your support team to help you? A mentor is someone who has your interests at heart and will spend time with you, discussing your development and making constructive suggestions. Reviewing your plan on a regular basis will help you to implement it. If you do not review regularly, the chances are that your plan will die a natural death. Nothing will have changed. Regular review with a mentor or peers means that time is set aside and importance is implied by your own and another's time commitment, if nothing else.

ON A FINAL NOTE ...

If *you* do not think that you are the best thing since sliced bread, worth time, energy and effort, why should anyone else? We are our own best asset and need to capitalise on what we have. But sadly, much of what we have goes unrecognised and undeveloped. We all have the seeds of charisma within us – let's not waste our potential. All my charismatic interviewees have worked hard at themselves and have all the Keys of Charisma in abundance. I hope that you have enjoyed reading their views as much as I enjoyed collecting them!

HOW TO MANAGE CHARISMATIC PEOPLE

6

Living with a charismatic person can be a bit like living with an unexploded bomb. You never know when – or why – they might go off. Like explosives, charismatics can produce positive or negative results. The problem is that what is negative to one is positive to another; and there's the rub.

We know that charismatic individuals are:

- Energetic
- Inspiring
- Influential within the workplace
- Quick thinking
- Often hard driven and ambitious.

They :

- Want to change things
- Challenge the *status quo*
- Often want to be 'top dog'.

They can be uncomfortable colleagues and are particularly uncomfortable to manage because they are non-conformist. They do not want to be the same as everyone else. And it is difficult not to worry that they might want your job! And yet these are the people who can achieve the quantum leap, designing and instituting change that can move an organisation ahead of its competitors, or drastically reduce costs by doing things differently. If they are socialised charismatics life isn't quite so painful for those around them, but if they are personalised charismatics life can be tough for everyone. The usual way of dealing with them is to get rid of them. This is what some of my interviewees said in response to a question asking them if they were difficult to manage:

> 'Oh yes, bloody *useless*! This is not just a question of being charismatic, but people like me are driven – that makes us sound miserable. We're not; we love being driven. We're strong horses, we like to have a clear sense of direction. That's why we like other strong leaders and are willing to put ourselves in harness. If you are driven towards an

objective and become single-minded, you can be a pest to live with and a pain to work for.'

Edwina Currie

'I always put it down to my Yorkshire upbringing. I know I can be obstinate but I think I am only obstinate mostly when I have good reason to be and I really do mind about something. I do try not to be awkward on purpose. I try to let go; one has to give all the time. I think I am quite tough, but is this being single-minded or obstinate? A bit of both maybe. It requires some soul searching!'

Mo Acland

'I've never been managed! I think I probably am difficult to manage if I'm being honest. I have very clear ideas about how things should be done. The people who've managed me best are people who have led me to believe that I was doing it my way, but they would sort of help shape the journey. Not many people have got that quality. Unless I feel that somebody is as good as I am, I won't tolerate being managed. I'm good at what I do and I have been managed by some men who I don't think have been as good as I am.'

Heather Rabbatts

'A man who is difficult to manage is often seen as having potential leadership qualities, like a skittish horse. But a woman who is difficult to manage is seen as trouble.'

Dame Rennie Fritchie

History tells us that most charismatics get the sack at some stage during their careers. Either that or they don't work for anyone else but set up their own businesses immediately. But charismatics are the wrong people to throw out. We need them. Managing charismatics requires two things:

- A very mature and confident approach by managers
- Individually tailored strategies to suit the individuals concerned.

AS A MANAGER ...

There are real differences between hierarchical and facilitative managers. The former can be represented by a pyramid, with the manager at the top cascading instructions downwards regardless of the views and talents of anyone lower down; the latter by a circle in which the manager is an enabler, facilitating the team to give of its best. Both have their strengths in appropriate situations. It is probably true to say that using a hierarchical style of management with charismatic individuals will result in either their leaving or being sacked from the organisation very quickly, or a failure to achieve a satisfactory contribution from them! The key to success lies in the approach you, the manager, take.

- What is your role? Are you 'top dog'?
- Do you see yourself as someone who has all the answers, and as 'she (or he) who must be obeyed'? Or do you see yourself as someone who is there to achieve the best answers by using the intelligence, expertise and experience of those on your team?
- Do you achieve your job sastifaction from making all the decisions and doing everything yourself, or do you get your satisfaction from helping others to do things?

The answers to these questions will indicate how successful you are likely to be in managing charismatic individuals.

What did my interviewees think?

'I suppose it does take a generous personality and a far-sighted person to recognise and indeed nurture people who were beneath you in the pecking order and who might well overtake one and zoom off into the stratosphere. If I was in an organisation with lots of people and levels of management, I would be delighted to be thought to be the one who actually encouraged so and so and gave them the push, the lift and the chance. It is a terrific privilege, not to mention a skill, to identify those who, with a little lift, would do great things.'

Mo Acland

'Human nature can lead down the road to the quiet life. For those who want that, I can see them being happier with compliant subordinates rather than those with independence of spirit. However, independence of spirit coupled with a better brain worries rather more complacent individuals and they can feel threatened by young upstarts.'

Lieutenant General Mike Jackson

'I think that if you've got someone on the team who's got leadership potential or charisma or whatever it is, they've got to be harnessed in such a way that they are working for you and not against you.

If you recognise you've got someone good, the best thing to do is to make sure that they are good and then give them a little area to work in.'

Christine Dipple

'I encourage charismatic individuals. I think people need frameworks. Our culture is one where they don't like to get things wrong, they certainly don't like to go outside of the remit that is given to them. They're uncomfortable with that and they like working to practice and procedures especially. With charismatic characters I feel I have to say, 'OK, I'll actually draw the parameters a little wider and give you the opportunity to step further out than I would normally', because they feel comfortable with that; it's all about making them feel comfortable. I think charismatic characters have to be monitored closely.'

Peter Sharpe

Levels of complexity

Dr Gillian Stamp at Brunel University has done some fascinating work which may be relevant to the issue of managing charismatic individuals. Her Career Path Appreciation and Levels of Work models suggest two things. First, that tasks and roles require different levels of complexity of decision-making. She lists seven levels. Level I indicates little complexity, although it may require a very high level of skill. Skilled technical and administrative jobs and artists are normally found at this level. At the other end of the continuum a level VII job indicates the maximum level of complexity, where an individual working in a role at this level has to manage complexity on a global level. Being CEO of a global corporation or a world-class political role would normally be at level VII. Middle management jobs are normally level III. Secondly, that individuals have the potential to operate comfortably at particular levels. An individual's capability can be measured against the requirement for each level. Put into roles at the wrong level, individuals can find themselves in situations with which they are not naturally comfortable. This may result in excessive stress, whether the role requires a higher or lower level of complexity of decision-making than they are comfortable with. The most important aspect of the model is that the level of complexity does *not* indicate better or worse, more or less important. It is about comfort zones and job requirements.

Ideally, individuals should have the opportunity to work at levels which match their current and potential levels. It would be very interesting to know whether individuals who have been identified as charismatic fall naturally into particular levels. I suspect that they might operate more comfortably with quite high levels of complexity; a number of them might be very comfortable at levels V and VI. This would indicate that they will probably be uncomfortable with many roles at middle management level and will want to change everything! The secret lies in putting them in the right jobs with the right supervision and development opportunities.·

HOW TO MANAGE CHARISMATIC INDIVIDUALS

- Give them space to grow and give of their best
- Ensure that they have a job or tasks which will stretch them
- Give them the authority and responsibility necessary to complete the task
- Ensure that you are available to help and advise whenever they need you
- Always take an interest
- Keep an open mind and be prepared to look at all their ideas seriously even when these ideas threaten your own security or undermine your own personal beliefs and practices
- Let them make mistakes but expect them to learn from them
- Let them 'fly'
- Encourage the qualities of socialised charismatics within them, eg involvement and care for others, service to others, etc.

I think that we should manage all staff like this, not just those who we think are charismatic. However, my experience tells me that it is even more important with potentially charismatic individuals. But it's not easy – we are all human!

I would be very interested to hear if anyone has any evidence of whether women are better than men as managers of charismatic individuals, or vice versa. Anecdotal evidence suggests that men are better at it than women which is interesting because the qualities required are probably more female in nature than male, and I would expect women to have more female qualities than men (here I make the assumption that both sexes have male and female qualities). However, this may be because women who have achieved senior management positions have done so against heavy odds and have had to adopt what we might think of as typically male behaviours. Dame Rennie Fritchie illustrated this point about male and female qualities for me:

'If I look at Nelson Mandela, he has charisma and he appears to epitomise the best of masculine and feminine qualities. There are some leaders that seem wholly masculine, who for a period of time may attract followers, but they are not necessarily charismatic people. I think it's about the blend and balance, I think it's about strength and softness.'

Lady Thatcher is not noted publicly for having encouraged anyone, charismatic or not, and her track record in promoting women was particularly poor. But then I suspect that her answers to the questions above might have been very different to those of Dame Rennie Fritchie, Christine Dipple and Peter Sharp.

LAST WORD

Far from being destructive unexploded bombs, charismatic individuals have the potential to make a very valuable contribution to organisations. This potential will only be realised by skilful, insightful managers and leaders who are more concerned with the success and needs of their organisation than with their own egos. Such managers take pleasure and delight in the success and development of those for whom they are responsible, and are mindful that they are accountable for creating environments in which all can flourish.

Everyone has a measure of charisma. It does not make sense to waste such a potentially valuable asset. With encouragement and support all of us, in whatever walk of life we find ourselves, can develop and enjoy this most exciting gift in ourselves and in others.

SUMMARY

- Charismatic individuals can be very difficult to manage
- They are frequently pushed out of organisations because they rock the boat
- They have the potential to make a substantial contribution to the organisation
- They need to be managed by mature, confident managers and given individually tailored opportunities with appropriate support
- Managers who manage charismatic individuals effectively
  — are very comfortable with the role of a facilitative manager
  — see their own success as coming through the success of those they manage and develop
  — are open to new ideas and suggestions all the time
- Charismatic individuals need
  — space to grow
  — support
  — authority and responsibility
  — opportunities to make mistakes and learn
  — encouragement to 'fly'.

APPENDIX – The survey

I carried out an informal survey, not a research project. However, the responses provide a very interesting insight into general perceptions of charisma. I sent my questionnaire to nearly 700 people and had a 35 per cent response rate. The recipients included:

Random selections from discrete groups
- Politicians
- Churchmen
- Management consultants
- Health service personnel
- Educators
- Chief executives
- Managers
- Journalists.

Personal and business contacts
This included individuals from many of the above groups, friends, retired people, young graduates and housewives, people in retail and other services.

Specifically targeted groups
- Sixth form students
- A group of individuals studying for their MBA
- Executive secretaries.

The questionnaire was designed to achieve qualitative information. I wanted personal definitions written in people's own words. The questionnaire asked people to say what they thought charismatic meant, who they felt had charisma (dead or alive), and who had it but could not be defined as a leader. In addition to age and occupation, respondents were also asked to identify qualities that described themselves best and least.

SUMMARY OF RESULTS

Those who received more than ten nominations as a charismatic individual in descending order:

Leaders – alive	Leaders – dead
Margaret Thatcher	Churchill
Nelson Mandela	John F Kennedy
Richard Branson	Hitler
Sir John Harvey Jones	Mahatma Gandhi
Michael Heseltine	Martin Luther King
Billy Graham	Jesus
Tony Blair	Charles de Gaulle
Pope John Paul II	Napoleon
	Queen Elizabeth I
	Alexander the Great
	Franklin Roosevelt
	General Montgomery
	Mother Theresa

Non-leaders – alive	Non-leaders – dead
Ian Botham	Marilyn Monroe
Paul Gascoigne	Diana, Princess of Wales
Richard Branson	Mother Theresa

- The definitions of charisma, many of which are quoted on pages 199–200, are very similar in nature to and reflect the Keys of Charisma
- There appears to be a general consensus in people's understanding of 'charismatic' which does not appear to be influenced by age or sex
- Fewer women than men were identified as charismatic: 145 out of a total of 720 people identified
- People under 20 identified many of the same people as charismatic as those over 20
- As many people over 50 identified current pop and sport stars as charismatic as did those under 50
- People who identified themselves as intelligent and well-educated did not appear to have difficulty in identifying charismatic individuals. This might contradict the American research which suggests that the more intelligent and better educated are less likely to identify individuals as charismatic. However, I make no formal claim for this as the research was not conducted with sufficient rigour and control

- Teachers were frequently remembered as being charismatic and having a significant influence on respondents
- Two individuals who were described as having suffered in Nazi concentration camps were identified as charismatic
- Respondents came from nine countries: UK, Ireland, South Africa, Belgium, France, Czech Republic, Australia, Sweden, Slovenia
- Four executive secretaries out of the 30 who responded nominated their managers
- The greatest number of responses from any single group came from managers and business consultants.

Quotes from questionnaires

What does 'charismatic' mean to you? And what is charisma?

Someone who is captivating with an 'energy field surrounding them'; provides a 'biochemical click', a feeling of having known them a long time; trust; aura.

Someone who is coercive in a subtle and endearing manner; leads through gaining commitment and loyalty, not compliance; charming, 'enchanting', articulate, flattering.

Someone who is able to change meaning for others, intellectually compelling, wonderful at sharing their vision.

Someone who is knowledgeable about most subjects without being a 'know-all'; the centre of attention without being an attention-seeker; and constantly couples these skills with an ability/desire to communicate at all levels of the social and economic spectrum.

Someone who is self-confident, at one with themselves, has a very amiable personality. Perhaps outspoken, entertaining.

Someone who is charming – gentle, but vibrant, not weak; who remembers your name, who considers the effects on people around, but who is a little 'different'. Individual.

Someone who is – ideally – transparent and full of integrity. Induces loyalty without being manipulative; realistic, able to create energy and enthusiasm by what she or he is saying or doing among others.

Someone who is able to gain people's respect and admiration easily. People are naturally drawn to them at times of crisis. People will tolerate their indiscretion.

Someone who is enthusiastic, gets people involved and enjoying themselves. Energetic and transfers energy; encouraging and pushing; takes initiative; leads by example.

Someone who is confident, and does not always follow the herd. He or she can take an unorthodox view on matters and lead others with flair and presence. Not always popular but usually with a great following. Opinionated; resilient; know what they want. A little bit of compassion in some cases.

Someone who is likeable, stylish and has presence that is very noticeable. Witty.

Someone who is lively, wakes me up, invigorating, larger than life.

Charisma is something you are born with (given as by God or by some supernatural power); you can have a tendency towards charisma which you cultivate with the right understanding. Charismatic people are like magnets, they attract other people. It seems that a charismatic person is sure of him or herself and knows his or her purpose in life. A charismatic person isn't necessarily aware of his or her ability to draw other people's attention. Charisma can be used for good or bad. A charismatic person can transmit energy with his or her voice, words, etc. You don't need to know a charismatic person personally in order to affect you. One can feel charisma through pictures or movies or even from the sound of someone's voice.

Someone who is or has a certain 'aura' – quite 'unique'. 'Riveting' in speech and action. Someone you do not want to leave, almost to the point of becoming 'adoration'.

Someone who is empathic, ebullient, enthusiastic.

Someone who is persuasive, magnetic, appealing – and charming. Firm and resolute in his or her actions. Never self-actualised, always striving for new goals – so restless and sometimes moody. Has command of language and uses it to good effect – sometimes to manipulate. Has ideas – good/bad.

Someone who is warm, friendly and genuine.

Someone who is inspiring with an attractive personality and a sense of vision they want to share without setting themselves up as a 'guru'.

Someone who is able to make a difference to a situation, with energy and presence.

Someone who is clear about their life mission and who radiates personal power; or someone who radiates personal power by speaking their truth and walking their talk.

Someone who is a leader, not a follower. Someone who inspires others by example. He or she is likely to be unconventional, have considerable 'style' and be able to soar above the boring and the average. He or she thinks for him or herself.

Someone who is bright and has a zest for life. Their energy and personality infuses those around them. Popular, respected and well liked – or hated!

Someone who is exciting to the senses by reason of beauty, intellect, spirituality, mental drive, physical ability – all or some or one of these.

Someone who is able to create a vision or purpose which people will follow, sometimes unquestioningly, through a personality which projects a 'spark' of vibrancy, originality and endearment to which people are drawn.

Someone who is magnetic, who excites blind obedience, unquestioning loyalty or adoration (a negative as well as a positive quality).

Someone who is well presented, and 'usually wearing a striking tie/silk handkerchief', etc; is confident in their views and believes in themselves – 'I might meet my equal but I won't meet anyone better'. A person with individual ideas and one not being led by others. Has the unconscious ability to make people believe in them!

Someone who is very much alive and projects this by means of a very attractive presence, be this either a friendly and positive projection or something more aggressive and less approachable.

Someone who is popular with the public.

Someone who is attractive and interesting in a way that may be hard to describe; someone who naturally draws people to them and enriches others by their physical presence. Can be good or evil.

Someone who is noticeable – good communicator, empathic, possessed of *admirable* qualities, mental and physical energy; an achiever, strongly principled but humane and kind. Must be generous of heart; able to motivate and carry people along. Pleasant looks and good general appearance helps. Also a touch of eccentricity/originality.

Someone who is able to make others share his or her enthusiasm, beliefs – like Robert Maxwell could.

Someone who is able to sway you to their will, someone with that bit extra, that little bit of magic (black or white) who is able to give you a surge of enthusiasm for their cause.

Someone who is respectful of human feelings, but also someone who commands personal respect through personal presence, interactions and achievements.

Someone who is able to excite interest, admiration or enthusiasm through powers of influence and dynamism. Usually a winner who displays brilliance in a simple, easy manner.

Someone who is remembered both for style and content, and whose style and content influences others to remember and recall by association.

Someone who is self-confident, attractive (in the broader sense of the word) and stylish. He or she is often flamboyant and somewhat eccentric, and is followed without having to ask people to follow.

Someone who is able to command respect and attention by their presence, and especially when they speak. This is often because their words seem relevant to oneself, and because it is easy to empathise with the person with charisma. They may also have one or more striking personal qualities.

Someone who is 'infectiously inspirational'. Literally: someone with personal 'power' who acts in a creative and benign way to exert influence over others. But in the organisational (business) context.

Someone who is able to convince one that they are capable of achieving more than they thought probable.

Someone who has an indefinable 'aura' about them – almost like the 'Ready-Brek glow'. Someone for whom you would walk through walls and scale mountains.

Someone who is energetic, entertaining and will always hold my attention without being boastful or full of self-importance. Someone who inspires me to achieve more because they make anything seem possible as demonstrated by their own achievements.

Someone who 'fills a room' with his or her personality.

Someone who is able to evoke feelings of passion and admiration, through the spoken word or through the demonstration of an outstanding talent, or some combination of these factors.

Someone who is charming and communicates ideas of interest well. Someone who intrinsically understands that before anyone else buys into their ideas *they* have to buy into them. Someone who doesn't *need* to be dictatorial because people *want* to follow them.

Someone who is charismatic has the charm to command attention and to enthuse for at least as long as they are present. Charisma has a short half life and in my book is beginning to be a slightly pejorative term. But charisma would assist most leaders who have the other necessary competences.

Someone who is warm, attractive (as a character, need not be physically attractive), generally male (!!), believable, followable – unlike John Major – interesting, relates to you (or you believe he could relate to you).

Someone who is like me!! Unique, different, bubbly, sparkling. Deep inner motivation for 'things' not associated with money. Americans call it 'spunk'. Indescribable, but you know it when you see it – enthusiasm and some magic dust.

Someone who is arresting in their style and manner and therefore memorable.

Someone who gives off confidence and an 'aura' – a degree of intrigue too.

Someone who is (a leader), self-confident, a good talker/speech-maker. I've noticed that charismatic people speak slowly – they know they have a good audience. They seem 'tall' irrespective of their actual height. Always strong personalities, focused.

Someone who has a vision, that is clearly communicated, that people 'buy into' because it is uplifting and gives them a noble cause that they are willing to make sacrifices for. Because they believe that ultimately they will achieve it and be better as a result.

Someone who is able to energise and dynamise people through his or her vision, enthusiasm and leadership skills – someone who cares! However, the word 'charismatic' is misused and misunderstood. The label has been given to the wrong people. Charisma is *not* a necessary characteristic of leadership skills!

Someone who is 'larger than life' and has the capacity to 'inspire' actions, feelings, fear or enthusiasm.

Someone who is able to convince others that he or she considers and understands the emotional needs of 'people' in the way that he or she behaves.

Someone who commands a presence through the force of their personality, having the ability to influence others without always being objective. Charisma is in the eye of the beholder.

Someone who is active, not reactive, and who has integrity matched by ability. Whose words are few but well-chosen, except when an uplifting speech is required.

Someone who is influential, powerful, respected, magnetic, a leader, fascinating, forceful, strong, inspiring, appealing, difficult to resist.

Someone who is outgoing, with a personality that draws you to them, someone you never forget.

Someone who is inspirational and an agent for change. Dangerous, too – which is, perhaps, why they are attractive. Visionary yet well grounded: without the latter there is a hollowness and the vision will not be embraced. Decisive, but their decisions are not always 'right' – dangerous again …

Someone who is inspiring and able to 'move' me; focused and clear about their direction; 'strong' yet vulnerable at the same time; passionate, unyielding and persistent by nature.

Someone who is persuasive, respected, admired, emulated, gifted.

Someone who has *presence*. Smiling, comfortable 'in his or her own skin', has intelligent eyes that look out widely, as if spanning the larger picture. Warm, enthusiastic, positive, assumes the best, not the worst. Able to relate to 'little people', appreciating their worth. Confident but always humble. Kind.

Someone who is able to get others to follow him or her through a series of obstacles, to continue to take them forward and to continue to be their leader/inspiration.

Someone who is worth being around, or watching, for stimulation and on the basis that one may learn something. Usually of a non-conformist nature and rarely uninteresting.

Someone who has a large persona, can motivate and lead people, communicate with staff at all levels, and who radiates positive energy.

Someone who is able to generate 'energy' in others. They inspire confidence (self and others). Excellent communicators (particularly of concepts and 'vision'). They live the words (American 'walk the talk').

I have never come across anyone I would describe in this way but I would expect it to mean someone who has a definite 'presence' and positive impact and is capable of using these to influence others and is aware of, and uses, that ability. For some reason, I would see it as a *male* attribute.

Someone who is perceived to be an individual who possesses leadership skills, commands attention and is revered wherever he or she may go.

Someone who exercises a compelling, hypnotic effect on those with whom he/she comes into contact.

Someone who is able to give a sense of excitement and pleasure when you are talking or listening to them. There is a natural attraction that makes any contact special and there is a particular interest in what the person is saying. Also they have the ability to suggest by their body language that they are interested in you and your views.

Someone who is firstly vibrant in the Holy Spirit.

Someone who almost has a personality before he or she opens his or her mouth.

Someone who is enormously attractive in either a positive or negative way – either intellectually or physically. Could therefore be repellent at the same time as being overwhelmingly fascinating.

Someone who is possessed of an indefinable magic. Positive characteristics that attract with clearly defined personality traits. Adversity perceived as a challenge, not a barrier. Ability to 'turn on' charm, worn almost like a halo. Able to influence.

Someone who is visionary, powerful but not necessarily pragmatic. They would usually have a strong sense of ethics though there are some obvious exceptions – perhaps ethical in their own terms. I think they would have a fairly powerful intellect, a good sense of style and, of course, they would have to have well-developed people skills.

Someone who is seen to have an aura as soon as they walk into a room. This is intangible but it provides a basis for inspiration for others. Magnetic. Able through their 'charisma' to recruit you as a follower. (I do not see it as always involving a verbal behaviour – often words are not part of charisma.)

Someone who is (i) able to perform, as described below, with other people; and (ii) able to stimulate me into doing something which either I had never thought of, or normally would not dream of either doing or being able to do! It is something to do with energy, enthusiasm, presence, sex appeal, positive encouragement, all of which is communicated to me as being the important person at that moment. This gives me strong self-belief – the urge to move mountains.

Someone who has an exceptional presence in a group; who commands attention; who inspires people to achieve things; who is a perfect role model for others; who generates immense respect; who is exceptionally creative.

Someone who is alive, energetic and warm. Can be gentle and unassuming but everyone is aware when they are in a room. Good communicator, good story-teller. Enthusiastic. Highly principled. Imaginative, creative. Self-confident, charming. Special. Someone you want to be near, often a teacher or a guru of some sort. Approachable, a leader, non-judgemental. Witty. Enigmatic. Curious and observant. Friendly, sympathetic, interested and interesting. Different. Encouraging. Intelligent, good.

Charisma is a very dangerous gift, and one which ruins you as soon as you realise you have it. It is especially dangerous for business people.

Someone who possesses a magnetic confident personality and who has the ability to display charm in their public persona. Someone who inspires with adventurousness and imagination and who has leadership qualities which attract others to their aims and objectives. Such a person is also ruthless in the pursuit of their aims and goals and is admired for this quality. Has a clear awareness of their strengths and weaknesses.

Someone who is a natural leader, whose head is held heavenward but whose feet are firmly on the ground. Whose character possesses an infectious enthusiasm for whatever they are involved in. One who honours the principle of St Paul's words found in Philippians 4, v8: 'Whatever is true, whatever is honourable, whatever is just.'

Someone who is followable, generally outgoing, brave, liked by her or his team, unemotional, a bit of a rebel.

Someone who is appealing to a number of people who believe he or she has a special message or special way of delivering it that makes him or her 'magnetic' and worth following, even at some personal cost.

Someone who is a good motivator, ie a happy-go-lucky person who could influence the glummest of people.

Someone who is compelling, charming, dominating but not domineering, the focus of attention in any room, capable of attracting attention, draws attention.

Someone who is powerful, visionary, a leader, single-minded, manipulative, driven, talented, energetic.

Someone who is different from the norm; stands out in a crowd.

Someone who is outstanding in his or her particular field. It is more than personality, though this is important. One immediately feels that here is someone, head and shoulders above his or her fellows, not necessarily achieved by outstanding ability but by a certain aura and leadership quality.

Someone who is giving off a sort of light, a sparkle. Makes one feel ready to agree or to follow. Gives one an agreeable feeling. Charisma is far more than 'charm'.

Someone who is talented and has an individual special flair. Someone who stands out because of having a different attractive style, prepared to take risks and is visibly different.

Someone who is enthusiastic enough to enthuse me.

Someone who is able to persuade others about issues whether they are accurate or not. Transcends the content and influences others through personal magnetism ... believable to others, not necessarily credible. The singer, not the song.

Someone who is energetic, enthusiastic, confident, knowledgeable, interesting, interested, positive, has presence, has influence, enigmatic, personality, receptive, articulate, expressive, animated, mysterious.

Someone who is able to make an uninteresting or even fearful situation much better.

Someone who is magnetic and has the ability to be the centre of attention without trying.

Someone who is fitted with a purpose, knows that he or she needs other people to effect the purpose and has empathy towards these other people.

Someone who is able to inspire others, fills people with enthusiasm and communicates well.

Someone who you warm to easily without much effort, someone who is practical and intellectual and someone who shows an interest in life and for life.

Someone who has peace of mind, actually has achieved some state of consciousness beyond most people.

Someone who is inspiring and who you would follow off a cliff!

The people I would describe thus appear to have the following in common: a particular 'look in their eye' and a direct gaze; fairly deep voice (hence more males than females!) with a 'compelling' tone; inner energy/dynamism/constant stream of ideas.

Someone who by actions shows what he or she is (not by big words). He or she is intelligent, positive, open-minded.

Someone who is glad to be alive, finds something good in everyone, is decisive but listens to all views, is persuasive but kind but, most importantly, treats everyone as an individual remembering their personal details, which makes them feel special.

Someone who is talented, outgoing, able to raise enthusiasm in and influence others.

Someone who is standing up for his or her beliefs, has a 'radiant' personality; gives the impression that he or she is very engaged and enthusiastic in what he or she does and can engage others; has a strong personal integrity.

Someone who is inspiring, good to listen to, attractive, fun, interesting, well-read, interested in other people, non-conventional.

Someone who is stylish, intelligent, charming; has flair.

Someone who draws people to them or controls them by their strength of character, dominance, fear. This can be through warmth, energy, enthusiasm, genuineness, empathy, looks, fear, dominance, power of their convictions, animal magnetism, character, vision, 'stage presence', mystique.

Someone who is a leader – usually for a cause (has a following); a free thinker – has a vision and aspires to it; prepared to see the issue through (whatever) to the end; aware of self-worth and it shows (aura); passionate – almost to the point of it being detrimental.

Someone who is able to influence people – because of their character they have special powers and qualities which make them appear (and prove to be) unique. I believe that someone who is charismatic is inspirational and can influence other people to do things because of *their* qualities.

Someone who is articulate and able to communicate and motivate others through their passion, drive and commitment. Able to stir up the emotions of others.

Someone with charisma is someone who: causes others to instantly take notice. It's a gift of instantly instilling power. Quality of being able to command respect. The charismatic have a kind of 'gravitas' (Greek). You have to listen. You feel impressed by them.

A personal quality enabling the possessor to influence, charm and inspire others. Charisma, like beauty, is in the eye of the beholder, someone able to exercise this power over one person would not necessarily have the same influence over others. An overwhelming desire to become involved, to be influenced and to be affected.

If I had any doubts about the contribution of charismatic personalities, they were quickly dispelled as I read through the questionnaire responses. Obviously, I could not include every response, but I have included both positive and negative responses in the same ratio as in the total received.

The responses provided me with a clear indication that overall charisma is a force for good. It is indeed a 'gift to other people'.

BIBLIOGRAPHY

Alder, Harry (1995) *Think Like a Leader*, Piatkus, London.

Barratt-Godefroy (1993) *How to Develop Charisma and Personal Magnetism*, Thorsons, London.

Bass, Bernard M (1985) *Leadership and Performance Beyond Expectations*, Free Press, New York.

Buzan, Tony and Keene, Raymond (1994) *Buzan's Book of Genius*, Stanley Paul, London.

Carling, Will and Heller, Robert (1995) *The Way to Win*, Little, Brown and Company, London.

Covey, Stephen R and Merrill, Roger A (1994) *First Things First*, Simon & Schuster Ltd, London.

Doran, Dr J (1858) *The History of Court Fools*, London.

Follett, Mary Parker (1949) *Freedom and Co-ordination: Lectures in Business Organisation*, L Urwick (ed), London.

Gardner, Howard (1995) *Leading Minds*, HarperCollins, London.

Goleman, Daniel (1996) *Emotional Intelligence*, Bloomsbury, London.

Hemery, David (1986) *In Pursuit of Sporting Excellence*, Willow Books: Collins, London.

Heron, John (1992) *Feeling and Personhood*, Sage Publications, London.

Heron, John (1993) *Group Facilitation*, Kogan Page, London.

Herrmann, Ned (1996) *The Whole Brain Business Book*, McGraw-Hill, New York.

Hodgson, P and J (1992) *Effective Meetings*, Century Business, London.

Howard, Roland (1996) *The Rise and Fall of the Nine O'Clock Service*, Mowbray, London.

Howell, Jane (1988) *Two Faces of Charisma: Socialised and Personalised Leadership in Organisations*, in Conger, J A and Kanungo, R N (eds), *Charismatic Leadership: The Elusive Factor in Organisational Effectiveness*. Jossey-Bass Inc, San Francisco and Oxford.

Jackson, Tim (1994) *Virgin King*, HarperCollins, London.

Kipling, R (1902) *Just So Stories*, Macmillan, London.

Machiavelli, Niccolo *The Prince*, English translation (1961) Penguin, Middlesex.

Shea, Michael (1993) *Personal Impact*, BCA: Sinclair-Stephenson, Reed Consumer Books Ltd, London.

Storr, Anthony (1989) *Churchill's Black Dog*, Collins, London.

Storr, Anthony (1996) *Fact of Clay*, HarperCollins, London.

Thompson, M (1966) *Churchill: His Life and Times*, Bookplan Odhams Books Ltd, Watford Herts.

Tzu, Sun (490BC) *The Art of War*, James Clavell (ed) (1981), Hodder and Stoughton, London.

Wilson, A N (1993) *The Rise and Fall of the House of Windsor*, Sinclair-Stephenson Reed Consumer Books, London.

Oxford Dictionary of Quotations, OUP, Oxford.

Concise Oxford Dictionary, OUP, Oxford.

FURTHER READING

Aburdene, Patricia and Naisbitt, John (1993) *Megatrends for Women*, Century, London.

Adair, John (1989) *Great Leaders*, Talbot Adair Press, Guildford.

Albert, P J and Hoffmann, R *We Shall Overcome*, Da Capo, New York.

Bowra, C M (1957) *The Greek Experience*, Phoenix, London.

Bryman, Alan (1992) *Charisma and Leadership*, Sage Publications, London.

Buzan, Tony and Gelb, Michael J (1995) *Lessons from the Art of Juggling*, Aurum Press, London.

Conger, Jay A and Kanungo, Ranbindra N (1988) *Charismatic Leadership*, Jossey-Bass Inc, San Francisco.

Covey, Stephen R (1994) *The Seven Habits of Highly Effective People*, Simon & Schuster Ltd, London.

Fayol, Henri (1916) *Administration Industrielle et Générale*, English translation, Pitman 1949, London.

Fisher, Mark (1991) *Millionaire's Book of Quotations*, HarperCollins: Thorsons, London.

Freemantle, David (1990) *Incredible Bosses*, McGraw-Hill, London.

Gregory, Richard L (ed) (1987) *The Oxford Companion to the Mind*, Oxford University Press, London.

Handy, Charles (1985) *Understanding Organisations*, Penguin Books, Middlesex.

Hollis, Christopher (ed) (1964) *The Papacy*, Weidenfeld and Nicolson, London.

Kenny, Ivor (1991) *Out on their Own*, Gill and Macmillan, Dublin.

Kershaw, Ian (1991) *Hitler*, Longman, London.

Koch, Richard and Godden, Ian (1996) *Managing Without Management*, Nicholas Brealey, London.

Kotter, John (1990) *A Force for Change: How Management Differs from Leadership*, Free Press, New York.

Mintzberg, Henry (1989) *Mintzberg on Management*, Free Press, New York.

Mintzberg, Henry (1994) *The Rise and Fall of Strategic Planning*, Prentice Hall International (UK) Ltd, Hertfordshire.

O'Connor, Joseph and Seymour, John (1990) *Introducing NLP*, Aquarian/Thorsons: HarperCollins Ltd, London.

Potter, Beverley (1985) *Ronin Strategies for Getting Ahead*, Personnel, March 1995.

Rodenburg, Patsy (1992) *The Right to Speak*, Methuen Drama, Reed Consumer Books Ltd, London.

Scott, Cynthia D and Jaffe, Denis T (1991) *Empowerment*, Kogan Page, London.

Tichy, Noel and Devine, Mary (1990) *The Transformational Leader*, John Wiley & Sons, New York.

Trice, H M and Beyer, J M (1986) *Charisma and its Routinization in Two Social Movement Organisations*, Research in Organisation Behaviour, Vol 8, pages 113–164.

Trompenaars, Fons (1993) *Riding the Waves of Culture*, Nicholas Brealey, London.

Wright, Peter (1996) *Managerial Leadership*, Routledge, London.

INDEX